The Baseball Addict's Trivia Book

*500 Questions and Answers
About Big League Baseball*

CHIP TRELLIX

The Baseball Addict's Trivia Book

500 Questions and Answers About Big League Baseball

Copyright 2021
Chip Trellix
Trellix Trivia Publishing

Baseball Stadiums

Did you know?

The diamond and all other areas that have painted and measured lines have to adhere to strict rules, but the rest of a ballfield is flexible.

The first night game in major league baseball history was played at Cincinnati's Crosley Field. It took place on May 24, 1935.

Fenway Park is the oldest Major League Baseball stadium and has been the home of the Boston Red Sox since 1912!

Even though Yankee Stadium is considered the "House that Ruth built," its original walls were constructed of extra durable concrete that Thomas Edison developed with a cement company he started in 1899.

Section 1
Questions 1-100

Copyright 2021
Chip Trellix and Trellix Trivia

"The designated hitter rule is like letting someone else take Wilt Chamberlain's free throws."   Rick Wise

1. How many players make up the roster of an MLB team?
A. 26
B. 24
C. 18
D. 36

2. Another name for the baseball manager is what?
A. At D Helm
B. Skipper
C. Leader
D. Head Man

3. You can enjoy nachos in a replica helmet at this park:
A. Angel Stadium
B. Petco Park
C. Target Field
D. Yankee Stadium

4. A team manager is known to apply the hook when he changes what?
A. Pitchers
B. His Shirt
C. Catchers
D. Center Fielders

"Rooting for the Yankees is like rooting for the house in blackjack."

Adam Morrow

5. The first player to claim 17 MLB Triple Crowns in 45 seasons is who?
A. Miguel Cabrera
B. Lou Gehrig
C. Tip O'Neill
D. Paul Hines

6. At 3 feet 7 inches he was the shortest player in a Major League Game:
A. Eddie Gaedel
B. Freddie Patek
C. Bobby Shantz
D. Stubby Magner

7. Sandy Koufax pitched for the Brooklyn / L.A. Dodgers:
A. Seven Seasons
B. Nine Seasons
C. Twelve Seasons
D. Fourteen Seasons

8. He was recruited by the MLB, the NFL, and the NBA, who was he?
A. Bo Jackson
B. Dave Winfield
C. Barry Bonds
D. Greg Maddux

"Progress always involves risks. You can't steal second base and keep your foot on first base."   Frederick B. Wilcox

9. What is the average bat speed of a MLB player?
A. 35 mph
B. 65mph
C. 80mph
D. 110 mph

10. A moon shot represents what?
A. High Home Run
B. High Cost for a Beer
C. The Climb to the Upper Seats
D. Rookie's First At-Bat

11. How many balls do you need to get a walk?

A. 2
B. 4
C. 5
D. 3

12. He appeared in 3 straight World Series with 3 different teams:
A. Don Baylor
B. Pete Rose
C. Willie Mays
D. Billy Earle

"Strikeouts are boring! Besides that, they're fascist. Throw some ground balls - it's more democratic."   Bull Durham

13. Three and two is known as a what?

A. Bathroom Location
B. Full Count
C. Score
D. Candy

14. A pitch that almost hits the batter is known as a what?

A. Brushback
B. Razor Face
C. Close Call
D. Lawsuit

15. According to John Fogerty -"Look at me, I can be _____."

A. Pitcher
B. Catcher
C. Center Field
D. Right Field

16. How many Division Titles have the New York Yankees won?

A. 3
B. 12
C. 14
D. 19

"The Mets have shown me more ways to lose than I even knew existed."
Casey Stengel

17. Who was traded by the L.A. Dodgers for being too small as a pitcher?
A. Whitney Ford
B. Johnny Cueto
C. Pedro Martinez
D. Tim Collins

18. What is the abbreviation for "Ground Into Double Play?
A. GIDP
B. DPGR
C. GNDP
D. GDB

19. In 2004 which player reached base three times more than at-bat?
A. Barry Bonds
B. Scott Rolen
C. Adrian Beltre
D. Mark Loretta

20. Since 2020 which one of these teams has gone the longest without winning the World Series?
A. Texas Rangers
B. Boston Red Sox
C. Baltimore Orioles
D. Seattle Mariners

"Baseball, it is said, is just a game. True, and the Grand Canyon is only a hole in Arizona. Not all holes, or games are created equal."

George Will

21. Base coaches help who?
A. Umpires
B. Catchers
C. Base Runners
D. Batters

22. Good Humor Fan Fest is found in which stadium?
A. Citi Field
B. Busch Stadium
C. T-Mobile Park
D. PNC Park

23. About how many baseballs do all 30 MLB teams use per season together?
A. 35,000
B. 48,000
C. 72,700
D. 918,000

24. Hank Aaron played for who when he beat Babe Ruth's record?
A. Miami Dolphins
B. New York Yankees
C. Los Angeles Dodgers
D. Atlanta Braves

"Baseball is the only place in life where a sacrifice is really appreciated."
Author Unknown

25. How many Gold Glove awards did Hank Aaron win in his career?
A. 3
B. 7
C. 8
D. 9

26. Another term for a hit is what?
A. Snag
B. Knock
C. Blast
D. Beamer

27. Who was the winningest pitcher in the 1960s with 191 wins?
A. Juan Marichal
B. Gary Peters
C. Dean Chance
D. Sam McDowell

28. The fastest inside-the -park home run was by who at 14.29 sec in 2014?
A. Kevin Kiermaier
B. Brandon Morrow
C. Jed Lowrie
D. Renato Nunez

"That rain delay was the most important thing to happen to the Chicago Cubs in the past 100 years. I don't think there's any way we win the game without it."
Anthony Rizzo

29. The first left-hander member of the 300 Win Club?

A. Eddie Plank
B. Jared Walsh
C. Brett Phillips
D. Jeffrey Springs

30. Who's 1994 start was pushed back for tattoo infection.

A. Alex Cole
B. Carl Everett
C. Jeff Juden
D. Kirk Gibson

31. A team not doing well is considered in a what?

A. Bad Way
B. Downplay
C. Dumps
D. Slump

32. First player who had their number retired by all MLB teams:

A. Babe Ruth
B. Mickey Mantle
C. Jackie Robinson
D. Hank Aaron

"The game is an island of activity amongst a sea of statistics."

Author Unknown

33. Bo Jackson's #697 ball card was in what company's Ad campaign?
A. Nike
B. Kool-Aid
C. Hertz
D. Under Armor

34. First U.S. President to throw the ceremonial first ball:
A. Abe Lincoln
B. William Howard Taft
C. Dwight D Eisenhower
D. John F Kennedy

35. A changeup is what?
A. Type of Pitch
B. Player Sub
C. Base Swap
D. Umpire Swap

36. Charlie Hustle was the nickname for which player?
A. Pete Rose
B. Charles Barkley
C. Charlie Chapman
D. Joe DiMaggio

"Baseball is a lot like life. It's a day-to-day existence, full of ups and downs. You make the most of your opportunities in baseball as you do in life."
Ernie Harwell (Sportscaster for 55 Years)

37. A pitcher that throws with a severe sidearm motion is known as a what?
A. Untapped Pitcher
B. Idiot
C. Side Armer
D. Submarine Pitcher

38. Which player was given a World War I draft deferment to support family?
A. Rogers Hornsby
B. Rabbit Maranville
C. Stan Spence
D. Mort Cooper

39. A ball hit on the ground producing an out is a what?
A. Sling low
B. Tapper
C. Groundout
D. Chip Shot

40. A first base runner, when more than one runner is on base is known as a what?
A. Runner Under Pressure
B. Fast
C. Lead Runner
D. Dodge Man

"My motto was always to keep swinging. Whether I was in a slump or feeling badly or having trouble off the field, the only thing to do was keep swinging."
Hank Aaron

41. Who was the first player to wear sunglasses?
A. Paul Hines
B. Joe DiMaggio
C. Lou Gehrig
D. Reggie Jackson

42. A home run hit with no runners already on base:
A. Solo Home Run
B. Runaway
C. Slap Out
D. Carry Over

43. How many teams did Jim Thome play for 1991 to 2012?
A. Three
B. Five
C. Six
D. Ten

44. First year Topps used unaltered photos for their base set:
A. 1938
B. 1945
C. 1957
D. 1963

"Baseball is dull only to dull minds."   Red Barber

45. This pitcher struck out five hitters in the 1934 All-Star game with a screwball:
A. Curt Davis
B. Hal Schumacher
C. Carl Hubbell
D. Lefty Gomez

46. Which pitcher had no right had?
A. Guy Hecker
B. Jim Colborn
C. Jim Abbott
D. Stubby Clapp

47. How many baseballs are used in a typical MLB game?
A. 4
B. 18
C. 36
D. 120

48. How many MLB players have hit 3 home runs on Opening Day?
A. 1
B. 2
C. 3
D. 4

"Never allow the fear of striking out keep you from playing the game!"
Babe Ruth

49. Accounted for nearly half of Phillies wins as pitcher in 1972.
A. John Coleman
B. Robin Roberts
C. Steve Carlton
D. George McQuillan

50. He recorded a hit for two teams in two cities on the same day.
A. Paul Waner
B. Ed Delahanty
C. Joel Youngblood
D. Wade Boggs

51. A tater is another word for what?
A. Foul Out
B. Foul Ball
C. Umpire
D. Home Run

52. Batting average is noted as this abbreviation on a scorecard.
A. AVG
B. BA
C. AVB
D. BAT

"It ain't over 'till it's over."   *Yogi Berra*

53. The penalty for a balk is known as a what?
A. Dead Ball
B. Loss
C. Rookie
D. Bad Signal

54. How many baseballs could Johnny Bench hold in one hand?
A. 7
B. 5
C. 9
D. 12

55. 2B is known as what on scorecards?
A. Second Inning
B. Pitcher
C. Double
D. Two Runs

56. Grover Cleveland Alexander elected to Hall of Fame in what year?
A. 1929
B. 1930
C. 1938
D. 1967

"More than any other American sport, baseball creates the magnetic, addictive illusion that it can almost be understood."

Thomas Boswell

57. A baseball game usually lasts for how many hours?
A. 3 Hours
B. 2 Hours
C. 4 Hours
D. 6 Hours

58. How many games did Wade Boggs reach base safely in 1985?
A. 39
B. 100
C. 112
D. 152

59. Extra innings are known as what?
A. Free Baseball
B. Waste of Time
C. Score Reset
D. Closure

60. The first player to score a hit in the newly formed National League:
A. Jim O'Rourke
B. Willie Mays
C. Ted Williams
D. Babe Ruth

"I said before the Series that a sweep wouldn't do it...It would have to be something epic. And that was epic, wasn't it?"

Tom Ricketts

61. How many baseball games are in a season?
A. 132
B. 150
C. 162
D. 183

62. A substitute base runner is known as what?
A. Helpmate
B. Showoff
C. Cheating
D. Pinch Runner

63. Baseball was invented in the 1800s with which rules?
A. Knickerbocker
B. Humdinger
C. Sasburger
D. Fletcheringer

64. A batter known to hit line drives everywhere is a what?
A. Maniac
B. Spray Hitter
C. Non-Disciplined
D. Slinger

"My whole philosophy is to broadcast the way a fan would broadcast."

Harry Caray

65. Houston Astros celebrate their history at this place:

A. Home Run Alley
B. Days of Old
C. Dugout Disco
D. Choo Choo Diner

66. How many decades did Nolan Ryan's career span?

A. Four
B. Three
C. Five
D. Seven

67. Players achieving "natural cycles" in "at bat" during a game?

A. 13
B. 14
C. 18
D. 21

68. What is Joe DiMaggio's hometown ?

A. Atlanta, GA
B. Brooklyn, NY
C. Martinez, CA
D. Chicago, IL

"Baseball is like church. Many attend, few understand."
Leo Durocher

69. AB is known as what on a scorecard?

A. Also Batted
B. Area Bunt
C. At-Bat
D. All Balls

70. A hitter that pulls to the side he is hitting:

A. Pull Hitter
B. Stiff Hitter
C. Direction Hitter
D. Dark Hitter

71. First umpire to use instant replay to reverse a call:

A. Fred Abbott
B. Charlie Chaplin
C. Frank Pulli
D. Harry Adams

72. Area that consists of the grass beyond infield is known as what?

A. Outfield
B. Holding Area
C. Sleeper Zone
D. Galley Way

"Every strike brings me closer to a home run."   Babe Ruth

73. How is sac fly abbreviated on a scorecard?

A. SF
B. SA
C. FA
D. FS

74. A player that never won MVP but stole over 800 bases is who?

A. Tim Raines
B. Ty Cobb
C. Rickey Henderson
D. Billy Hamilton

75. Who was the first to sign a contract worth one million dollars per season?

A. Nolan Ryan
B. Ty Cobb
C. Joe Crotty
D. John Smoltz

76. He was a lifetime Kansas City Royal for 21 years?

A. George Brett
B. George Jones
C. George Harrison
D. Ty Cobb

*"Love is the most important thing in
the world, but baseball is pretty good too."*
Yogi Berra

77. A pickle is known as what?

A. A Concession Snack

B. A Rundown

C. Catcher's Mistake

D. Loss

78. Fenway Park is known for its what?

A. Hot Dogs

B. Fudge

C. Autograph Alley

D. Underground Bar

79. How many no-hitters were thrown in the 2012 regular season?

A. 12

B. 7

C. 21

D. 4

80. CS stands for what on a scorecard?

A. Caught Stealing

B. Climatic Stop

C. Cut Stands

D. Crisis Stop

"Yesterday's home runs don't win today's games."   *Babe Ruth*

81. Another word for an easily handled pitch is what?
A. Salad
B. Elementary Ball
C. Passive Pitch
D. Sleeper

82. How many pitchers have recorded over 600 complete games?
A. None
B. Fourteen
C. Two
D. Eight

83. Coaches use what to hit to infielders during practice?
A. Fungo Bats
B. Clubs
C. Mallets
D. Cane Poles

84. A curve ball is also known as what?
A. Uncle Charlie
B. Widow Maker
C. Cheat Throw
D. Sidewinder

"You know, a lot of people say they didn't want to die until the Red Sox won the World Series. Well, there could be a lot of busy ambulances tomorrow."
Johnny Damon

85. A strong long-distance hitter is known as a what?
A. Power Hitter
B. Freak
C. Lucky Man
D. Straight Shooter

86. Who is the first fielder to throw out three runners at home plate?
A. Jack McCarthy
B. Greg Maddux
C. Steve Carlton
D. Catfish Hunter

87. The Cy Young was first awarded in what year?
A. 1879
B. 1956
C. 1960
D. 1971

88. Who holds the record for stealing home plate?
A. Ty Cobb
B. Babe Ruth
C. Pete Rose
D. Rickey Henderson

"You never know what's going to happen... And that's the fun of it! That's what baseball is all about."
Keiichi Arawi

89. Metal-halides are used for what in baseball stadiums?
A. Kill Roaches
B. Clean Toilets
C. Light Stadium
D. Transfer Concessions

90. Who won three consecutive CY Young Awards in his career?
A. Sandy Koufax
B. Pete Townshend
C. Jim Palmer
D. Greg Maddux

91. Baseball is played on a geometrical shaped field known as a what?
A. Diamond
B. Star
C. Rectangle
D. Octagon

92. A pitcher that pitches an entire game is known to have a what?
A. Stressful Day
B. Bonk Game
C. Complete Game
D. Sweet Game

"It's hard to beat a person who never gives up."   Babe Ruth

93. Dodger Stadium opened in what year?
A. 1955
B. 1963
C. 1962
D. 1945

94. Prior to 2013, who was the grand slam leader?
A. Lou Gehrig
B. Grey Hunter
C. Pete Rose
D. Babe Ruth

95. A ball hit back to the pitcher is what?
A. Dangerous
B. Comebacker
C. Return Shot
D. Boomerang

96. An organic restaurant can be found in this ballpark:
A. AT&T Park
B. Wrigley Field
C. Petco Park
D. Fenway Park

"Playing baseball for pay-home run. Teaching kids to play the game-priceless."
Jack Perconte

97. Which player won a World Series MVP for a losing team?
A. Bobby Richardson
B. Mike Scott
C. Jeffrey Leonard
D. Richard Petty

98. Hank Aaron grew up in what city?
A. Mobile
B. New York
C. Houston
D. Montgomery

99. A splitter is a type of what?
A. Coach
B. Inning
C. Dugout
D. Pitch

100. Games played is represented by what abbreviation on scorecards?
A. G
B. GP
C. GA
D. PG

World Series Facts & Fun
Did you know?

1903: The first World Series was played.

1904: Guess what? There was no series played this year.

1921: The Yankees won the first of an MLB record 27 World Series titles.

1949-53: The Yankees won a record five consecutive World Series.

1955: The World Series MVP Award was first time given to Brooklyn's Johnny Podres.

1969: The Yankee's Don Larsen pitched the only perfect game in World Series history.

1992: The World Series was played outside of the United States for the first time, with the Toronto Blue Jays defeating the Atlanta Braves 6-0.

The Seattle Mariners are the only current franchise team in MLB baseball to not appear in the World Series.

Section 2
Questions 101-200

"Things could be worse. Suppose your errors were counted and published every day, like those of a baseball player."

William Alexander

101. The Baker Bowl was once known as what?
A. National League Park
B. Sun Chips Stadium
C. Cactus Park
D. Wayward Grounds

102. What player missed a start by getting bitten by his mother-in-law's dog?
A. Joe DiMaggio
B. Tony Gwynn
C. David Cone
D. Barry Bonds

103. The fastest baseball pitch recorded for a woman was what?
A. 73mph
B. 84mph
C. 69mph
D. 64mph

104. The Bullpen Market can be found here:
A. Safeco Field
B. Wrigley Field
C. Yankee Stadium
D. Miller Park

"I'd rather be the shortest player in the Majors, than be the tallest in the minors."
Freddie Patek

105. The Baseball Hall of Fame was built in what year?
A. 1901
B. 1927
C. 1939
D. 1948

106. Interact with this friend at Tropicana Field centerfield:
A. Stingray
B. Snake
C. Electric Eel
D. Swordfish

107. Who wore his entire birthday of May 17 on back of uniform?
A. Carlos May
B. Buckshot May
C. Dave May
D. Derrick May

108. The Gold Glove Award was first awarded in what year?
A. 1957
B. 1932
C. 1963
D. 1945

"If you get three strikes, not even the best lawyer in the world can get you off."
Bill Veeck

109. Which pitcher holds the all-time record for hitting the most home runs while playing the pitcher's position?

A. Wes Ferrell
B. Bob Lemon
C. Warren Spahn
D. Tim Anderson

110. The Green Monster is in which ballpark?

A. Fenway Park
B. Yankee Stadium
C. Petco Park
D. Wrigley Field

111. The 1927 Yankee lineup was known as what?

A. Murderers' Row
B. Motley Crew
C. Dynasty Bunch
D. Green Wallers

112. Stadium with "Federal Donuts" for concessions:

A. Citizens Bank Park
B. Fenway Park
C. Dodger Stadium
D. Wrigley Field

"I never took the game home with me. I always left it in some bar."
Bob Lemon

113. How many record All-Star games were played by Hank Aaron?
A. 12
B. 14
C. 25
D. 28

114. Who won the MVP in both American and National Leagues?
A. Frank Robinson
B. Willie Mays
C. Peter Benchley
D. Lou Gehrig

115. Mickey Mantle's nickname was what?
A. Mistro
B. Big Mike
C. The Mick
D. Michelangelo

116. If a batter commits a whiff, they have what?
A. Gotten Fined
B. Walked
C. Struck Out
D. Fouled Out

"I knew when my career was over. In 1965 my baseball card came out with no picture."   Bob Uecker

117. Who is the only pitcher in history to throw a no-hitter on his birthday?
A. George Mullen
B. Sandy Koufax
C. Randy Johnson
D. Roger Clemens

118. No RBI was awarded in this year's All-Star game:
A. 1945
B. 1958
C. 1967
D. 1968

119. Ride a Carousel at this ballpark:
A. Comerica Park
B. AT&T Park
C. Wrigley Field
D. Petco Park

120. The most popular ballpark food is what?
A. Pickles
B. Pizza
C. Peanuts
D. Hot Dogs

"Winning is the most important thing in my life, after breathing. Breathing first, winning next."   George Steinbrenner

121. The most innings pitched in a season was pitched by who?

A. Will White
B. John Clarkson
C. Guy Hecker
D. Babe Ruth

122. Hit forty home runs & hit .400 or better in single season?

A. Hank Aaron
B. Rogers Hornsby
C. Joe DiMaggio
D. Lou Gehrig

123. In 1962 which pitcher struck out the first six batters he faced?

A. Pete Richert
B. Bob Purkey
C. Don Drysdale
D. Sandy Koufax

124. If runners are on second and third bases, they are in what?

A. Scoring Position
B. In Easy Outs
C. Pinch Runners
D. Base Steelers

"Baseball must be a great game to survive the fools who run it."
Bill Terry

125. Small theatre provides history of Kansas City Royals where?
A. Kauffman Stadium
B. Mile High Stadium
C. Wrigley Field
D. Truist Park

126. Ozzie Smith was known as what?
A. The Wizard of Oz
B. Oz Man
C. Mr. Oz
D. Oz Fest

127. Who was the last pitcher to legally throw a spitball?
A. Brooklyn Robins
B. Roger Clemens
C. Burleigh Grimes
D. John Smoltz

128. Who is the record holder for the most RBIs in a season?
A. Hack Wilson
B. Willie Mays
C. Barry Bonds
D. Jackie Robinson

"The best thing about baseball is there's no homework."

Dan Quisenberry

129. Who struck out Ruth and Gehrig in succession & banned from MLB?
A. Jackie Mitchell
B. Ed Wells
C. Cy Warmoth
D. Hub Pruett

130. The quickest game in MLB took place Oct 28, 1919 and lasted how long?
A. 48 Minutes
B. 51 Minutes
C. 78 Minutes
D. 84 Minutes

131. The most career shutouts by a pitcher is who?
A. Walter Johnson
B. Babe Ruth
C. Cy Young
D. Greg Maddux

132. The phrase "walk-off home run" did not apply before this year:
A. 1898
B. 1915
C. 1920
D. 1988

"With the money I'm making, I should be playing two positions."
Pete Rose

133. Rod Carew was named All-Star how many times?
A. Three
B. Eighteen
C. Twelve
D. Twenty-Nine

134. The first and only 500 game winner is which pitcher?
A. Cy Young
B. Babe Ruth
C. John Smoltz
D. Shane Bieber

135. The first ball card to show the stat - "Saves by Pitcher" was manufactured by what company ?
A. Upper Deck
B. Topps
C. Donruss
D. Panini

136. The name for baseball fans in the early days?
A. Cranks
B. Tin Hats
C. Sprinklers
D. Chunks

"Baseball is a skilled game. It's America's game-it and high taxes."
Will Rogers

137. Pitch delivered after a full count.

A. Payoff Pitch
B. Pleasing Pitch
C. Puffed Pitch
D. Sandbagger

138. Who was the oldest to hit a home run at 47 years 240 days old?

A. Ty Cobb
B. Ted Williams
C. Julio Franco
D. Pete Rose

139. In 2004 this player reached base more times than at-bat?

A. Barry Bonds
B. Mark Rogers
C. Wade Townsend
D. Matt Bush

140. How many times did Babe Ruth reach base safely in 1923?

A. 379
B. 400
C. 500
D. 521

"I became a good pitcher when I stopped trying to make them miss the ball and started trying to make them hit it."
Sandy Koufax

141. What year did the L.A. Angels begin to play in the MLB, as an expansion team to the American League?
A. 1940
B. 1958
C. 1961
D. 1972

142. The COP is also known as what?
A. Sweet Spot
B. Rub Point
C. Peer Zone
D. Cost of Pitchers

143. A great stadium with something located in center field for fans:
A. Coors Field
B. Fenway Park
C. Dodger Stadium
D. Yankee Stadium

144. The most All-Star games played by Hank Aaron was how many?
A. 14
B. 18
C. 25
D. 31

"If God wanted football played in the spring, he would not have invented baseball." — Sam Rutigliano

145. The record for most road losses in a season is 101 by this team:
A. Houston Astros
B. Miami Marlins
C. Cleveland Spiders
D. Boston Red Sox

146. Who holds the record for the most outfield assists in a single season ?
A. Mickey Mantle
B. Orator Shafer
C. Ty Cobb
D. Barry Bonds

147. Number of hits recorded by MLB record holder Pete Rose.
A. 2356
B. 3458
C. 2369
D. 4256

148. If you win the league championship you win what?
A. The Pennant
B. The Crown
C. The Stick
D. The Gavel

"Baseball is reassuring. It makes me feel as if the world is not going to blow up."   *Sharon Olds*

149. The most expensive autographed baseball sold for how much?
A. $ 191,200
B. $ 178,200
C. $ 150,321
D. $ 632,369

150. In baseball a fight that breaks out is known as a what?
A. Spectacle
B. Rhubarb
C. Sight for Sore Eyes
D. Bout

151. Most hits in a season as of 2004 was by who?
A. Ichiro Suzuki
B. Todd Helton
C. Jim Thome
D. Marcus Giles

152. This player was struck by Lightning in 1914 while catching a fly ball:
A. Sherry Magee
B. Charlie Hanford
C. Dan Adams
D. Red Murray

"He hits from both sides of the plate. He's amphibious."

Yogi Berra

153. The last major park to install lights was which stadium?
A. Wrigley Field
B. Safeco Field
C. Truist Park
D. Fenway Park

154. Who is the only pitcher to pitch to a horse on a TV show in 1963?
A. Sandy Koufax
B. Don Cardwell
C. Don Drysdale
D. Jim Maloney

155. Monument Park is to Yankee fans as Heritage Park is to?
A. Indian Fans
B. Braves Fans
C. Marlins Fans
D. Phillies Fans

156. How many stitches make up a major league baseball?
A. 108
B. 123
C. 145
D. 600

"The two good things in life are friends and a strong bullpen."
Bob Lemon

157. The player with the most career MLB hits is who?
A. Pete Rose
B. Willie Mays
C. Joe DiMaggio
D. Hank Aaron

158. Johnny Bench played what position for the Cincinnati Reds?
A. First Base
B. Catcher
C. Shortstop
D. Right Field

159. Set record for most career complete games?
A. Cy Young
B. Randy Johnson
C. Greg Maddux
D. Babe Ruth

160. One of the best left-handed pitchers in history was who?
A. Lefty Grove
B. Poncho
C. Slim Whitman
D. Sugar Ray

"Baseball is a fun game. It beats working for a living" *Phil Linz*

161. Rickwood Field is located where?
A. Birmingham
B. Atlanta
C. Detroit
D. Miami

162. The only player killed by a major league pitch by Carl Mays?
A. Ray Chapman
B. Ty Cobb
C. Dizzy Dismukes
D. Joe McGinnity

163. People knew Joe DiMaggio as what?
A. A Jerk
B. Joe Baby
C. Joltin' Joe
D. Jack Rabbit

164. Who was known as Mr. October?

A. Reggie Jackson
B. Hank Aaron
C. Pete Rose
D. Babe Ruth

"Willie Mays' glove is where triples go to die."   Jim Murray

165. What was Hank Aaron's nickname ?
A. Hammerin' Hank
B. Hit Man
C. Hammerman
D. Iron Arm

166. The "Hill" is what?
A. Pitcher's Mound
B. Coaches Bathroom
C. Concession Stand
D. First Base

167. John Smoltz's age when returning to rotation after injury?
A. 29
B. 34
C. 39
D. 43

168. 7 Fountains erupt at this stadium when the home team hits a home run:
A. Fenway Park
B. Petco Park
C. Coors Field
D. Truist Park

"Finish last in your league and they call you idiot. Finish last in medical school, and they call you doctor."   Abe Lemons

169. How much did Mark McGwire's 70th home run baseball sell for?
A. Three Million
B. One Hundred Thousand
C. Five Hundred Thousand
D. Eight Hundred Thousand

170. Longest hitting streak was 56 games set in 1941 by who?
A. Stan Musial
B. Lou Gehrig
C. Joe DiMaggio
D. Babe Ruth

171. How many times did Topps feature Tommy Davis on a different team from 1966 -1972
A. Two
B. Three
C. Seven
D. Nine

172. PB stands for what on scorecard?
A. Passed Ball
B. Placed Ball
C. Pretty Bad
D. Play Ball

"It's Deja-vu, all over again." Yogi Berra

173. How many teams did Rusty Staub have 500 hits with?
A. Eight
B. Six
C. Four
D. Ten

174. Natural frequency of a wooden bat is what?
A. 250 Hertz
B. 195 Hertz
C. 300 Hertz
D. 305 Hertz

175. Record holder for cosecutive no-hitters:
A. Johnny Vander Meer
B. Sandy Koufax
C. Babe Ruth
D. John Smoltz

176. The longest MLB game consisted of how many innings.
A. 14
B. 20
C. 25
D. 6

"In a way an umpire is like a woman. He makes quick decisions, never reverses them, and never thinks you are safe when you are out."
Larry Goetz

177. Miami Marlins Park has a nightclub named what?
A. The Clevelander
B. Out Stack
C. Bumbling
D. Higher Life

178. Which catcher holds the record catching for 25 innings?
A. Carlton Fisk
B. Johnny Bench
C. Mike Piazza
D. Roy Campanella

179. Who is the only pitcher to strike out Tony Gwynn three times in a game?
A. Tom Noland
B. John Smoltz
C. Cy Young
D. Bob Welch

180. Most career wild pitches thrown was by who?
A. Tony Mullane
B. Jack Morris
C. Joe Niekro
D. Mark Baldwin

"Baseball is the only major sport that appears backward in a mirror."
George Carlin

181. HP stands for what on scorecard?
A. Hit by Pitch
B. High Pitch
C. Hard Pitch
D. Hung Pitch

182. The first World Series took place in what year?
A. 1903
B. 1921
C. 1935
D. 1950

183. The highest level of seats in a stadium?
A. Nosebleed Seats
B. Nest Seats
C. Eagle Eye View
D. Heaven

184. The only player to have worn all 4 of New York's franchises' uniforms:
A. Casey Stengel
B. Rinaldo Ardizio
C. Elston Howard
D. Whitley Ford

"Our chances of winning, I've got to believe are really, really small when you score one run in eighteen innings."
Clint Hurdle

185. The most career sacrifice bunts record holder for the US Major League is who ?
A. Eddie Collins
B. Chipper Jones
C. Greg Maddux
D. Grey Hunter

186. How many times did Nolan Ryan strike out 163 different batters?
A. Ten
B. Twelve
C. Eighteen
D. Twenty-One

187. Only player to hit the warehouse behind Camden Yards:
A. Ken Griffey Jr.
B. Hank Aaron
C. Babe Ruth
D. Barry Bonds

188. What stadium did Pope John Paul II lead mass in 1987?
A. Dodger Stadium
B. Fenway Park
C. Yankee Stadium
D. Coors Field

"Don't try to be a hero. Try to be a winner."   George Brett

189. Who is the record holder for the most career no-hitters?
A. Nolan Ryan
B. Mariano Rivera
C. Andy Pettitte
D. John Smoltz

190. The San Diego Padres stadium is known as what?
A. Petco Park
B. Wolf Den
C. Canyon Stadium
D. Cactus Site

191. Larry "Chipper" Jones is best known for what position?
A. Third Baseman
B. First Baseman
C. Catcher
D. Right Field

192. How many sides does Home Plate have?
A. Three
B. Five
C. Four
D. Eight

"There are peaks and valleys in this game. Right now, we are in a valley - Death Valley."
Kirby Puckett

193. Rule 7.08i denotes what?
A. Order of Base Steals
B. Putting Out a Base Runner
C. Foul Balls
D. Eligible Outfielders

194. Who is the only pitcher in majors to record both 200 wins and 150 saves?
A. Cy young
B. Sandy Koufax
C. John Smoltz
D. Nolan Ryan

195. The batting order of players is also known as what?
A. Payroll
B. Call Up
C. Roll
D. Lineup

196. Jimmy Piersall suffered from what?
A. Lung Cancer
B. Bipolar Disorder
C. Vertigo
D. Polio

"The key to being a good manager is keeping the people who hate me away from those that are still undecided."   Casey Stengel

197. What year did both the New York Giants and the Philadelphia Phillies pitch the idea of pinstripes?

A. 1905
B. 1911
C. 1932
D. 1956

198. The ballpark that contains fire pits is known as what ballpark?

A. Target Field
B. PNC Park
C. Oracle Park
D. Dodger Stadium

199. Manny's is known for what type of food at PNC Park in Pittsburg?

A. Pulled Pork BBQ
B. Soul Food
C. Fish & Chips
D. Italian Ice Cream

200. How many teams make up the playoffs?

A. Seven
B. Eleven
C. Ten
D. Fourteen

Baseball Trading Cards

Did you know?

One of the most popular baseball trading cards manufacturers is Topps. They also are the same manufacturer of "Garbage Pail Kids" trading cards.

Topps employee Sy Berger is responsible for the design of trading cards. He was honored with his own trading card in 2004.

A pristine 1952 Mickey Mantle rookie card can sell for well over $1 million!

Topps is noted for having printed the "world's largest Baseball Card." In 2013, as a promotional stunt, they printed a 60 foot by 90-foot card. It featured Detroit Tigers 1B Prince Fielder and it was presented at the Tigers spring training camp in Lakeland, Florida.

A "1909 T206 HONUS WAGNER" card sold for $6.6 million on Aug 16, 2021.

Section 3
Questions 201-300

"We just made too many wrong mistakes."   Yogi Berra

201. The Beatles played their first U.S. summer tour concert here:
A. Shea Stadium
B. Fenway Park
C. Wrigley Field
D. Dodger Stadium

202. Had a statue erected of himself in his backyard:
A. Ivan Rodriguez
B. Johnny Bench
C. Jonathon Lucroy
D. Wilson Contreras

203. The worst injury a pitcher can have is a what?
A. Labrum Tear
B. Athlete's Foot
C. Crotch Itch
D. Charlie Horse

204. The number worn by Sandy Koufax & Elston Howard in 1963 MVP Awards?
A. 32
B. 44
C. 45
D. 62

"I watch a lot of baseball on the radio."   Gerald Ford

205. This pitcher's wife filed for divorce the night before his perfect 1956 World Series game:

A. Don Larsen
B. Bob Buhl
C. Whitney Ford
D. Lew Burdette

206. The abbreviation BK is used for what on scorecards?

A. Balk
B. Bad Attitude
C. Batter Up
D. Ball

207. Which of these is not a type of pitch?

A. Knuckleball
B. Cutter
C. Snotball
D. Eephus

208. Jim Hunter's nickname was which of these fish?
A. Catfish
B. Sword Fish
C. Bone Fish
D. Tuna Fish

"A hot dog at the game beats roast beef at the Ritz."
Humphrey Bogart

209. This pitcher won a game with only one pitch:

A. Noland Ryan
B. Greg Maddux
C. Ken Ash
D. Babe Ruth

210. He threw out three runners at home plate in the same inning:

A. Jack McCarthy
B. Randy Johnson
C. Tom Seaver
D. Cy Young

211. He hit the longest home run ever hit in San Francisco:

A. Mel Ott
B. Willie McCovey
C. Matt Williams
D. Barry Bonds

212. When a batter is called out on strikes, he is what?

A. Caught Looking
B. Sorry
C. Sad
D. Has Wondering Eyes

"I'd be willing to bet you, if I were a betting man, I have never bet on baseball."
Pete Rose

213. Pitched perfect game in World Series history in 1956?

A. Frank Lary
B. Sal Maglie
C. Don Larsen
D. Clem Labine

214. The Rubber Game in a series is known as what?

A. Deciding Game
B. Costly Game
C. Watchful Game
D. Split Game

215. The Texas Rangers formed, and was known as the Washington Senators in what year?

A. 1945
B. 1961
C. 1962
D. 1970

216. The first year that a sitting president attended a World Series game:

A. 1908
B. 1910
C. 1915
D. 1963

"Slump? I ain't in no slump... I just ain't hitting."   Yogi Berra

217. This player was banned from baseball for life, for betting on games while managing his own team:
A. Bryan Price
B. David Bell
C. Pete Rose
D. Dusty Baker

218. Who was enshrined in the Baseball Hall of Fame in its first class?
A. Ray Brown
B. Jack Chesbro
C. Christy Mathewson
D. Chief Bender

219. What is a pitched ball traveling at high speed called ?
A. Pea
B. Terror
C. Blackout
D. Marble

220. What position did Josh Gibson play?
A. Right Field
B. Pitcher
C. Shortstop
D. Catcher

"As a nation, we are dedicated to keeping physically fit - and parking as close to the stadium as possible." Bill Vaughan

221. Which team wore the first baseball uniforms?
A. Knickerbockers
B. White Stockings
C. Beaneaters
D. Trolley Dodgers

222. What is a one base hit known as?
A. Sorry
B. Single
C. Slip
D. Skane

223. What are the only 2 positions that are allowed or required to use a Mitt?
A. Pitcher & Third Base
B. Right Field & Catcher
C. Third Base & Shortstop
D. Catcher and First Base

224. This pitcher's fastball was clocked at 102 mph.
A. Greg Maddux
B. Randy Johnson
C. Walter Johnson
D. Bob Feller

"Little League baseball is a very good thing because it keeps the parents off the streets." Yogi Berra

225. Where is the Keystone Sack located on a baseball diamond?
A. First Base
B. Second Base
C. Third Base
D. Home Plate

226. Who was a fourteen time All-Star and won a Gold Glove?
A. Ernie Banks
B. Earl Gibbons
C. Ernest T Bass
D. Ken Ash

227. What year was a game called in New York in the sixth inning due to snowball fights amongst fans?
A. 1907
B. 1912
C. 1934
D. 1981

228. Which inning is the Baseball Anthem played at every MLB game?
A. Third
B. Fifth
C. Seventh
D. Ninth

"If you don't succeed at first, try pitching."   Jack Harshman

229. Which Mickey was nicknamed "Black Mike"?
A. Mickey Cochrane
B. Mike Tyson
C. Mickey Mantle
D. Michael Morse

230. What disease forced Lou Gehrig to retire?
A. Amyotrophic Lateral Sclerosis
B. Alcoholism
C. AIDS
D. Yellow Fever

231. Which manager was ejected from a record 91 games?
A. Tommy Lasorda
B. Earl Weaver
C. Joe Maddon
D. Bobby Cox

232. What Character was inspired by Yogi Berra?
A. Yogi Bear
B. Scooby Doo
C. Deputy Dog
D. Peppa Pig

"Who is this Baby Ruth and what does she do?"

George Bernard Shaw

233. This player had seven straight seasons with at least 200 hits:
A. Boz Scaggs
B. Wade Boggs
C. Paul Waner
D. Ty Cobb

234. What ball field was built on land owned by Babe Ruth's father's saloon?
A. Camden Yards
B. Fenway Park
C. Safeco Park
D. Petco Park

235. How many consecutive games from 1982 to 1998 did Cal Ripken Jr. play in ?
A. 1,125
B. 1,902
C. 2,490
D. 2,632

236. What is the oldest MLB ballpark?
A. Fenway Park
B. Wrigley Field
C. Yankee Stadium
D. Dodger Stadium

"There are only two seasons: winter and baseball."   Bill Veeck, Jr

237. Who was the owner that wanted Day-Glo orange baseballs used during games?

A. Charles O. Finley
B. John Fisher
C. Ted Lerner
D. Charles Johnson

238. What type of mascot is "Billie the Marlin?"

A. A Fish
B. A Snake
C. A Bobcat
D. An Otter

239. What number did Babe Ruth wear?

A. 13
B. 30
C. 3
D. 34

240. This player had a voting percentage of (98.5%) in the Hall of Fame in 2007?

A. Cal Ripken Jr.
B. Randy Johnson
C. Babe Ruth
D. Honus Wagner

"I think I throw the ball as hard as anyone. The ball just doesn't get there as fast."   Eddie Bane

241. This pitcher had 363 wins (6th most in MLB) & a lifetime ERA of 3.09?
A. Warren Spahn
B. John Smoltz
C. Sandy Koufax
D. Mike Mussina

242. He died the same day as actor Christopher Reeve.
A. Ken Caminiti
B. Tim Worrell
C. Carl Crawford
D. Eric Byrnes

243. "The Rocket" was a nickname for this player:
A. Roger Clemens
B. Johnny Bench
C. Hank Aaron
D. Cy Young

244. What is the area between the foul poles and including the foul poles called?
A. Danger Zone
B. Easy Street
C. Fair Territory
D. Ecstasy

"The funny thing about these uniforms is that you hang them in the closet, and they get smaller and smaller."
Curt Flood

245. Which player injured himself with his own false teeth?
A. Clarence Blethen
B. Lenny Dykstra
C. Giancarlo Stanton
D. Ty Cobb

246. What position did Lou Gehrig play?
A. Pitcher
B. First Base
C. Catcher
D. Centerfield

247. Which company produced the Frank Thomas "No Name on Front" #414 baseball card?
A. Keebler
B. Topps
C. Upper Deck
D. Panini

248. Joel Zumaya missed three games in 2006 doing what?
A. Cutting a Tree Down
B. Playing Guitar Hero
C. Grilling Out
D. Washing His Car

"There ain't much to being a ballplayer, if you're a ballplayer."

Honus Wagner

249. Ty Cobb was known as what?
A. The Georgia Peach
B. Mississippi Plum
C. Cabbage Kid
D. Cotton Head

250. What is the max numerical slugging percentage, even though no player has ever recorded this feat?
A. Four Thousand
B. One Hundred
C. Five Hundred
D. One Thousand

251. Which player gave up three years of his baseball career to fight in WWII?
A. Hank Greenberg
B. George S Patton
C. Gomer Pyle
D. Bob Feller

252. What year were wax pack cads first offered by the Topps baseball card company?
A. 1952
B. 1970
C. 1985
D. 1990

"The way to catch a knuckleball is to wait until the ball stops rolling and then pick it up."   Bob Uecker

253. Which is considered the hot corner on a baseball field?
A. Where Sun Shines
B. Third Base
C. Shortstop
D. Pitcher's Mound

254. Where did Jackie Robinson play his first MLB game ?
A. Ebbets Field
B. Wrigley Field
C. Fenway Park
D. Shea Stadium

255. Which position wears the "Tools of Ignorance"?
A. Catcher
B. Umpire
C. Pitcher
D. Shortstop

256. What do the Hall of Fame members Bob Gibson, Lou Brock and Fergie Jenkins have in common?
A. They all formed a Barber Shop Quartet
B. They all played for the Harlem Globetrotters
C. They all have run marathons
D. They all have shaken hands with the then sitting president

"Us ballplayers do things backward. First we play, then we retire and go to work."   *Charlie Gehringer*

257. Who was the first player in NL history to hit 2 grand slams in 1 game?
A. Tony Cloninger
B. Bill Duggleby
C. Red Ruffing
D. Wes Ferrell

258. Which pitcher faced Roger Maris, Mark McGwire, and Barry Bonds?
A. Nolan Ryan
B. Cy Young
C. Randy Johnson
D. Jerry Reuss

259. This type of pitch nearly hits the batter:
A. Brushback
B. Skanker
C. Twin Snout
D. Razor Face

260. What year was Frankie Frisch voted into the Hall of Fame?
A. 1921
B. 1947
C. 1951
D. 1960

"Think! How the hell are you gonna think and hit at the same time?"
Yogi Berra

261. Tom Seaver won the World Series in 1969 with which team?
A. New York Mets
B. Boston Red Sox
C. Pittsburgh Pirates
D. Los Angeles Dodgers

262. Which city has oldest baseball stadium still in use by the MLB?
A. Boston
B. Atlanta
C. Chicago
D. Kansas City

263. Which base is considered the most stolen base in MLB?
A. Second Base
B. One Not Guarded
C. Home Plate
D. First Base

264. What do batters use to increase a bat's weight during practice?
A. Anvil
B. Huge Bolt
C. Donut
D. Block

"The baseball mania has run its course. It has no future as a professional endeavor." Cincinnati Gazette editorial, 1879

265. How did the Brooklyn Dodgers get their name?
A. Dodging Trolley Cars
B. Dodging Taxes
C. Draft Dodging
D. Dodging Balls

266. When was Frankie Frisch voted into the Baseball Hall of Fame?
A. 1930
B. 1931
C. 1947
D. 1970

267. Which former Pro football player became an AL MLB umpire in 1936?
A. Ham Allen
B. Cal Hubbard
C. Nick Altrock
D. Andy Anderson

268. What year was the wild card rule introduced to baseball?
A. 1994
B. 1997
C. 1999
D. 2001

"The Hall of Fame is for baseball people. Heaven is for good people."

Jim Dwyer

269. Which company sponsors the Gold Glove Award?

A. Topps
B. Mattel
C. Rawlings
D. Nike

270. Two or three players on base are known as what?
A. Ducks on the Pond
B. Lucky Dudes
C. Miracle Boys
D. Happy Go Luckies

271. Which of the following will bat second and play at their stadium?
A. Tried Team
B. Blast Team
C. Home Team
D. Big Team

272. Distance between bases on a typical MLB baseball field?
A. 63 feet
B. 75 feet
C. 90 feet
D. 110 feet

"There are two theories on hitting the knuckleball. Unfortunately, neither one of them works."
Charley Lau

273. Which pitcher made 24 quality starts out of 25 games in 1994?
A. Tom Glavine
B. Robin Roberts
C. Tim Keefe
D. Greg Maddux

274. Tom Seaver was also known as what?
A. Tom Terrific
B. Tommy Boy
C. Tom Thumb
D. Thomas the Train

275. This ballpark is home to a famous beer:
A. Miller Park
B. Yankee Stadium
C. Wrigley Field
D. Safeco Field

276. This player died in a tragic plane crash, who was he?
A. Roberto Clemente
B. Yadier Molina
C. Francisco Lindor
D. Willi Mays

"All I remember about my wedding day in 1967 is that the Cubs lost a double-header."   George F. Will

277. The Barrelman mascot belongs to which team?
A. New York Yankees
B. Atlanta Braves
C. Baltimore Orioles
D. Milwaukee Brewers

278. This team managed to turn two triple plays in 1990 into a loss:
A. Minnesota Twins
B. Cincinnati Reds
C. Houston Astros
D. Atlanta Braves

279. What year did two deaf players face each other in a game?
A. 1902
B. 1942
C. 1951
D. 1963

280. Which of these pitchers did not play in the 1980s?
A. Jack Morris
B. Cy Young
C. Ron Guidry
D. Bob Welch

"Alan Sutton Sothoron pitched his initials off today."
Anonymous, St. Louis Newspaper

281. The third base umpire position is known as what?

A. Rocking Chair
B. Eagle Eyes
C. Jumper
D. The Wall

282. Which baseball glove company did not originate in the USA?

A. Nokona Athletic Goods
B. Rawlings
C. Wilson
D. Mizuno

283. What's the most valuable baseball card in the world?

A. 1909 T206 Honus Wagner
B. 1963 Pete Rose
C. 1951 Mickey Mantle
D. 1916 Babe Ruth

284. Which number did Derek Jeter wear, and it also was retired in 2017 by the New York Yankees?

A. #2
B. #4
C. #17
D. #23

"Never root for a team whose uniforms have elastic stretch waistbands." — Susan Sarandon

285. What is the batter after the on-deck batter called?
A. In the Hole
B. Scared
C. Out of Place
D. Impatient

286. In the 1977 World Series, what player hit three home runs in a row at Yankee Stadium?
A. Reggie Jackson
B. Barry Bonds
C. Peter Jennings
D. Ty Cobb

287. Opening day 2018 for the Atlanta Braves produced which mascot?
A. Blondie
B. Blooper
C. Blinkie
D. Blandman

288. The record of 29 postseason home runs belongs to whom?
A. Hank Aaron
B. Johnny Bench
C. Babe Ruth
D. Manny Ramirez

"Third ain't so bad if nothing is hit to you."   Yogi Berra

289. Who was the youngest inductee elected into the hall of fame in 1972, at the age of 36?
A. Sandy Koufax
B. Johnny Mize
C. Duke Snider
D. Yogi Berra

290. The Second Baseman is what number in the scorebook?
A. 3
B. 4
C. 7
D. 9

291. Which one of these baseball cards was featured in the movie "The Accountant?"
A. T206 Honus Wagner
B. 1916 Babe Ruth
C. 1909 Joe Jackson
D. 1968 Nolan Ryan

292. The record for the player most often hit by a pitch is who?
A. Hughie Jenning
B. Johnny Bench
C. Barry Bonds
D. Curt Schilling

"We know we're better than this, but we can't prove it."
Tony Gwynn

293. Baxter the Bobcat belongs to which team?
A. Atlanta Braves
B. Los Angeles Dodgers
C. Houston Astros
D. Arizona Diamondbacks

294. What number is the right fielder on a scorecard?
A. 9
B. 4
C. 6
D. 3

295. What is it sometimes called when a batter makes ideal contact with the ball ?
A. Sober
B. On the Screws
C. In the Grove
D. Focused

296. Which base is known as the dish?
A. Home Plate
B. Third Base
C. Second Base
D. First Base

"Well, it took me 17 years to get 3,000 hits in baseball, and I did it in one afternoon on the golf course."   Hank Aaron

297. Which player missed his start in 2001 because he stabbed himself while opening a package?
A. Clayton Kershaw
B. Adam Eaton
C. Mike Trout
D. Mookie Betts

298. Where does the mud come from that is used to rub on all baseballs before games?
A. Texas
B. Miami
C. Alaska
D. New Jersey

299. Which player ran the bases backward to celebrate his 100th home run?
A. Jimmy Piersall
B. Joe DiMaggio
C. Reggie Jackson
D. Ty Cobb

300. What is the name of the Toronto Blue Jays mascot?
A. Avery
B. Evert
C. Ace
D. Jay

Baseball Movies

The Pride of The Yankees (1942)

Take Me Out to the Ball Game (1949)

The Jackie Robinson Story (1950)

Fear Strikes Out (1957)

Damn Yankees (1958)

Bang the Drum Slowly (1973)

The Bingo Long Traveling All-Stars & Motor Kings (1976)

The Bad News Bears Go to Japan (1978)

Field of Dreams (1989)

A League of Their Own (1992)

Rookie of the Year (1993)

Angels in the Outfield (1994)

The Life and Times of Hank Greenberg (1998)

Air Bud: Seventh Inning Fetch (2002)

The Rookie (2002)

Fever Pitch (2005)

The Perfect Game (2009)

Moneyball (2011)

A Mile in His Shoes (2012)

Million Dollar Arm (2014)

Section 4
Questions 301-400

Copyright 2021
Chip Trellix and Trellix Trivia

"They say some of my stars drink whiskey, but I have found that the ones who drink milkshakes don't win many ball games."
Casey Stengel

301. Who set record for most career triples?
A. Sam Crawford
B. Pete Rose
C. Eddie Collins
D. Tommy Leach

302. Mickey Mantle was what number?
A. 7
B. 12
C. 10
D. 9

303. Another name for a fastball is what?
A. Blow Torch
B. Windy City
C. Cheese
D. BB Shot

304. Who was the first deaf baseball player?
A. William Hoy
B. Ed Dundon
C. Curtis Pride
D. Dick Sipek

"Baseball is not life. It is fiction, a metaphor. And a ball player is a man who agrees to uphold that metaphor as though lives were at stake."
David James Duncan

305. He called his last game as home-plate umpire in "56" World Series:
A. Don Larsen
B. Bill Klem
C. Babe Pinelli
D. Jocko Conlan

306. Who had 45 career four-hit games?
A. Pete Rose
B. Tony Gwynn
C. Mark McGuire
D. Mickey Mantle

307. What is an "Ace"?
A. Home Run
B. Single
C. Starting Pitcher
D. Catcher

308. What is a beanball known as?
A. Line Drive
B. Foul in Stands
C. Pitch that Hits Batter in Head
D. Warm Up Fake Ball

"On the baseball diamond, if nowhere else, America was truly a classless society. DiMaggio's grace embodied the democracy of our dreams."
David Halberstam

309. The first domed stadium in the world was what?

A. Astrodome
B. Rogers Centre
C. Marlins Park
D. Minute Maid Park

310. Who holds record for most All-Star selections at a total of 25?

A. Willie Mays
B. Barry Bonds
C. Hank Aaron
D. Greg Maddux

311. Who was the only player appearing with a mustache in the Topps T206 set of cards?

A. John Titus
B. Willy Wonka
C. Ty Cobb
D. Rube Manning

312. What number is associated with Derek Jeter?

A. 5
B. 2
C. 9
D. 11

"Baseball really is a glorified game of throw and catch. And if you don't have guys who throw it really well, you can't compete for long."
Tucker Elliot

313. Who was named as MVP in the 1999 World Series?
A. Mariano Rivera
B. Greg Maddux
C. El Duque
D. Darryl Strawberry

314. Who was the only player to play for same team in 3 different cities?
A. Eddie Mathews
B. Frank Sinatra
C. Clayton Kershaw
D. Nick Anderson

315. Who was an All-Star nine times in his career?
A. Jimmie Foxx
B. Jamie Foxx
C. Redd Foxx
D. Pete Rose

316. This player hit his only home run 20 min after Neil Armstrong walked on moon.
A. Harmon Killebrew
B. Gaylord Perry
C. Hank Aaron
D. Willie McCovey

"Baseball is a game with a lot of waiting in it; it is a game with increasingly heightened anticipation of increasingly limited action."
John Irving

317. He was a 14-time All-Star winner and suspended twice for steroids use?

A. Alex Rodriquez
B. Willie Mays
C. Barry Bonds
D. Ty Cobb

318. What number did Wade Boggs wear for Boston?

A. 10
B. 15
C. 4
D. 26

319. Who is the first player to use a helmet?

A. Roger Bresnahan
B. Joe DiMaggio
C. Ty Cobb
D. Buster Mills

320. "Rookie of the Year" first time award was given:

A. Cy Young
B. Babe Ruth
C. Willie Mays
D. Jackie Robinson

"Oh, to be a center fielder, a center fielder – and nothing more."
Philip Roth

321. Who set the record for the most RBIs (40), in World Series play?
A. Mickey Mantle
B. Reggie Jackson
C. Ty Cobb
D. Pete Rose

322. What Position did Joe Morgan play?
A. Catcher
B. 2nd Baseman
C. Right Field
D. Pitcher

323. Who is the first left-hander member of the 300 Win Club?

A. Lefty Grove
B. Eddie Plank
C. Warren Spahn
D. Sandy Koufax

324. This team outhit Cleveland in 1920 series but still lost (8-1):
A. New York Yankees
B. Brooklyn Dodgers
C. Chicago Cubs
D. Boston Red Sox

"A no-hitter is a freaky thing,' Tweet said. 'Most of the greatest pitchers never pitched one. It's a combination of a lot of little accidents."
Duane Decker

325. Who is record holder for consecutive no-hitters?
A. Johnny Bench
B. Joe DiMaggio
C. Pete Rose
D. Johnny Vander Meer

326. What does DP stand for?
A. Double Play
B. Deep Pattern
C. Deck Practice
D. Digital Press

327. Who was walked more times than any other player?
A. Barry Bonds
B. Mel Ott
C. Eddie Yost
D. Ted Williams

328. What does "Around the Horn" refer to?
A. Triple Play
B. Hit to Center Field
C. Concessions Run
D. Press Announcement

"Baseball is also a game of balance."   Stephen King

329. Outfielder Mookie Betts of the Sox was fearful of what?

A. Shells
B. Snakes
C. Rust
D. Clowns

330. Who was the major league's oldest rookie?

A. Satchel Paige
B. Babe Ruth
C. Pete Rose
D. Diomedes Olivo

331. What does "RISP" stand for?

A. Runs in Standing Pit
B. Runners in Scoring Position
C. Required Infield Starting Position
D. Risked in Player Struck

332. Who was the only sportswriter elected to the Baseball Hall of Fame?

A. Henry Chadwick
B. Mike Lupica
C. Red Smith
D. Peter King

"A ballplayer spends a good piece of his life gripping a baseball, and in the end, it turns out that it was the other way around all the time."
Jim Bouton

333. The mascot "Paws" likes to hang out with which team?

A. Cleveland Indians
B. Atlanta Braves
C. New York Yankees
D. Detroit Tigers

334. Who is the first pitcher to win 3 or more Cy Young Awards?
A. Steve Carlton
B. Randy Johnson
C. Nolan Ryan
D. Sandy Koufax

335. Which pitcher threw the first no-hitter in Coors Field?

A. Tom Glavine
B. Randy Johnson
C. Hideo Nomo
D. Greg Maddux

336. He was one of 29 players to appear in MLB games in 4 calendar decades.

A. Ken Griffey Jr.
B. Barry Bonds
C. Yogi Berra
D. Whitney Ford

"I don't rate them, I just hit them."   Willie Mays

337. Hit 53 of the 212 home runs in 2013 for Orioles?
A. Dylan Bundy
B. Chris Tillman
C. Chris Davis
D. Jason Hammel

338. Who struck out 26% of batters he faced in the 1970s?
A. Nolan Ryan
B. Steve Carlton
C. Tommy John
D. Jim Palmer

339. What position did Reggie Jackson play?
A. Shortstop
B. 3rd Baseman
C. Left Fielder
D. Right Fielder

340. The first mascot to exist in human form was what?
A. Billy the Marlin
B. Homer the Brave
C. Lou Seal
D. Mr. Met

"It is dangerous to spring to obvious conclusions about baseball or, for that matter, ball players. Baseball is not an obvious game."
Roger Kahn

341. Who stole 138 bases in 1887?

A. Rickey Henderson
B. Honus Wagner
C. Hugh Nicol
D. Eddie Collins

342. Who was banned for life from Baseball Hall of Fame?
A. Pete Rose
B. Jackie Gleason
C. Mickey Mantle
D. Joe DiMaggio

343. Who was the first player to hit 54 home runs in one season?
A. Pete Rose
B. Reggie Jackson
C. Babe Ruth
D. George Foster

344. This Cleveland mascot celebrated its twenty-ninth birthday July 29th of 2019.

A. Hankker
B. Big Snot
C. Slider
D. Fatso

"Fenway is the essence of baseball." *Tom Seaver*

345. Who played in 3 straight World Series for 3 different teams?
A. Barry Bonds
B. Amos Otis
C. Don Baylor
D. Troy Glaus

346. Who holds record for most triples in a lifetime?
A. Sam Crawford
B. Jimmy Hoffa
C. Hank Aaron
D. Honus Wagner

347. Rafael Palmeiro tested positive for drugs when?
A. 1999
B. 2005
C. 2012
D. 2018

348. Who was the first woman to do play-by-play for the Chicago White Sox?
A. Mary Shane
B. Mary Jane
C. Betty Boop
D. Julia Child

"Deep down, it's all baseball, no matter what kind of geometrical shape you play it with."

Vernon D. Burns

349. Who was the Dodger announcer when Hank Aaron hit record home run?
A. Red Barber
B. Joe Davis
C. Ernie Harwell
D. Vin Scully

350. Who struck out both Bobby Bonds and Barry Bonds?
A. Nolan Ryan
B. Randy Johnson
C. John Smoltz
D. Greg Maddux

351. Who was known to "shut the door" if their team wins?
A. Closing Pitcher
B. Owner
C. Manager
D. First Baseman

352. What are the main colors of the Baltimore Orioles Mascot?
A. Blue & White
B. Red & Green
C. Orange & Black
D. Purple & Gold

"If there are any curses left in baseball, they are all on the north side of Chicago."   Tucker Elliot

353. Which team was the first to introduce Salaries for its players?
A. Cincinnati Red Stockings
B. Boston Beaneaters
C. New York Yankees
D. Baltimore Orioles

354. What number does Ozzie Smith wear?
A. 5
B. 1
C. 12
D. 31

355. Who was inducted to Hall of Fame as a second baseman in 1990?
A. Joe Morgan
B. Robin Yount
C. Tom Seaver
D. Vic Willis

356. Which left-handed pitcher had the second-most lifetime strikeouts?
A. Cole Hamels
B. Patrick Corbin
C. Steve Carlton
D. Mike Minor

"They were both Mets fans, and the hopelessness of that passion had created a bond between them."
Paul Auster

357. Who played 2632 games straight?

A. Cal Ripken Jr.
B. Babe Ruth
C. Pete Rose
D. Jackie Robinson

358. One of the best pitching rotations in history in the 1990s?
A. Houston Astros
B. Miami Marlins
C. Cleveland Indians
D. Atlanta Braves

359. Who said, "We made too many wrong mistakes?"
A. Yogi Berra
B. Joe DiMaggio
C. Johnny Dickshot
D. Cal McLish

360. Earned Runs is abbreviated as what?

A. EAR
B. RE
C. EA
D. ER

"I see great things in baseball. It's our game - the American game."
Walt Whitman

361. Who was the first National League player to hit 500 home runs?
A. Cy Young
B. Mel Ott
C. Pete Rose
D. Bryce Harper

362. First African American pitcher in World Series game?
A. Satchel Paige
B. Flip Wilson
C. Bob Gibson
D. Vida Blue

363. First A. L. pitcher with 2 complete Game victories in 1 day?
A. Frank Owen
B. Patrick Corbin
C. Jack Flaherty
D. Justin Verlander

364. Which team were the first to wear numbers on the back of their jerseys?
A. Cleveland Indians
B. Houston Astros
C. New York Yankees
D. Baltimore Orioles

"Baseball is a good thing. Always was, always will be." Stephen King

365. What year did Hank Aaron appear on a Wheaties box?
A. 1971
B. 2002
C. 2012
D. 2014

366. Another word for home run is what?
A. Dinger
B. Missile
C. Arrow
D. Loft

367. Who was part of Yankees dynasty that won 5 Straight World series?

A. Johnny Mize
B. Jerry Seinfeld
C. Yogi Berra
D. Alex Rodriguez

368. Which player played 3 different positions and was 7 times All-Star?
A. Johnny Bench
B. Willie Mays
C. Craig Biggio
D. Barry Bonds

*"I've always loved baseball. Ever since 6th grade,
I was geared to becoming a baseball writer."*
Scott Miller

369. The First World Series to have a game scheduled at night?
A. 1968
B. 1970
C. 1971
D. 1976

370. Who had a single season (1924) record batting average of .424?
A. Rogers Hornsby
B. George Kelly
C. Bob Meusel
D. Babe Ruth

371. Who was 10x Silver Slugger and Hall of Famer Catcher?
A. Mike Piazza
B. Johnny Bench
C. Yadier Molina
D. Jonathon Lucroy

372. Who was an eight-time All-Star pitcher for Cleveland Indians?
A. Bob Feller
B. Mel Harder
C. Addie Ross
D. Orel Hershiser

"Worrying about things you can't control is a waste both on the baseball field and in life."
Tom Swyers

373. Orbit belongs to which team?

A. Atlanta Braves
B. Houston Astros
C. Baltimore Orioles
D. Los Angeles Angels

374. First baseball player to appear on a Wheaties cereal box (1934):

A. Mel Harder
B. Babe Ruth
C. Lou Gehrig
D. Mickey Mantle

375. Bag is another word for what?

A. Base
B. Fertilizer
C. Out
D. Umpire Brush

376. What number did Tom Seaver wear for the Mets?

A. 8
B. 16
C. 22
D. 41

"I've fallen in love with baseball."   Nick Jonas

377. Who coined the term "sabermetrics"?
A. Bill James
B. Babe Ruth
C. Roger Clemens
D. Willie Mays

378. Which World Series was never actually played?
A. Second
B. Fifth
C. Tenth
D. Fifteenth

379. Found not guilty of lying to congress on all 6 counts in 2012?
A. Roger Clemens
B. Neil Armstrong
C. Sandy Koufax
D. Mike Trout

380. Who had ten career steals of home plate?
A. Babe Ruth
B. Pete Rose
C. Ty Cobb
D. Rickey Henderson

"There's not an American in this country free until every one of us is free."

Jackie Robinson

381. Which team had 4 thirty home run hitters in the same season?
A. Atlanta Braves
B. Chicago Cubs
C. New York Yankees
D. Los Angeles Dodgers

382. Who played for Cincinnati Reds from 1967 to 1983 as catcher?
A. Johnny Bench
B. Joe Torre
C. Lance Parrish
D. Hank Aaron

383. Who was the player that won a silver medal as a speed skater in the 2014 Winter Olympics?
A. Eric Hosmer
B. Eddy Alvarez
C. Matt Olson
D. Evan White

384. What type of mascot is "Captain", the mascot of the Texas Rangers?
A. Dog
B. Horse
C. Whale
D. Chipmunk

"There are three types of baseball players: those who make it happen, those who watch it happen, and those who wonder what happens."
Tommy Lasorda

385. What does CS stand for?

A. Concession Stand
B. Catchers Spot
C. Caught Stealing
D. Carry Stats

386. Who had Nine All-Star Awards and Eight Silver Slugger Awards?

A. Vladimir Guerrero
B. Willie Mays
C. Dazzy Vance
D. Herb Pennock

387. When a batter hits a ball between 2 outfielders it is a what?

A. Snake Run
B. Power Hit
C. Gapper
D. Money Shot

388. The first home run by a pitcher in World Series happened when?

A. 1845
B. 1908
C. 1920
D. 1945

"I don't want to be one of those great players who never made the Series."
Rickey Henderson

389. Who was a 2-time World Series winner, and 2 times winner of the CY Young Award?
A. Bob Gibson
B. Randy Johnson
C. Greg Maddux
D. Babe Ruth

390. Who is the first member of the 3000 hit Club?
A. Pete Rose
B. Cap Anson
C. Ty Cobb
D. Mickey Mantel

391. Which pitcher said that he threw his June 12, 1970 no-hitter while under the influence of LSD?
A. Steve Carlton
B. Doc Ellis
C. Catfish Hunter
D. Tommy John

392. Which pitcher had the same amount of hits as he did wins throughout his career?
A. Warren Spahn
B. Goose Goslin
C. Zach Wheat
D. Charlie Jamieson

"Fans don't boo nobodies."   Reggie Jackson

393. Who had his number 42 retired by every team in baseball in 1992?
A. Jackie Robinson
B. Cy Young
C. Babe Ruth
D. Rogers Hornsby

394. Who was nicknamed Mr. October?
A. Reggie Jackson
B. Willie Mays
C. Sandy Koufax
D. Pete Rose

395. Who was the first athlete of any sport to be on the cover of Sports Illustrated?
A. Eddie Mathews
B. Pee Wee Herman
C. Mark Spitz
D. Mark Kauffman

396. Who hit a home run into a Tuba?
A. Hank Aaron
B. Barry Bonds
C. Willie Stargell
D. Tony Gwynn

"There may be people who have more talent than you, but there's no excuse for anyone to work harder than you."
Derek Jeter

397. Which player had the highest career batting average of .366?

A. Ty Cobb
B. Ted Williams
C. Barry Bonds
D. Stan Musial

398. What do both Lance Armstrong & Alex Rodriguez share in common?

A. They Both Dated a Girl Named Sue
B. They Both Love to Bike
C. The Both Went to Same High school
D. They Both Failed Drug Test

399. The mascot Stomper would be at home where?

A. T-Mobile Park
B. Target Field
C. RingCentral Coliseum
D. Target Field

400. Which name is not an actual name of any MLB player?

A. Wambsganss
B. Mientkiewicz
C. Snarrelgasinski
D. Kuntz

1892: The first U.S. president to attend a baseball game: Benjamin Harrison.

1890: The first Triple-Header was played: Brooklyn Bridegrooms swept the Pittsburgh Alleghenys.

1904: The first World Series to Ever Be Canceled.

1965: First player to hit a home run in the Houston Astrodome: Mickey Mantle (1965) in front of 47,876 fans.

April 6, 1973: The first designated hitter (DH): Ron Blomberg.

Section 5
Questions 401-500

Copyright 2021
Chip Trellix and Trellix Trivia

"I'm the straw that stirs the drink." Reggie Jackson

401. This player was known for peeing on his hands to make them tougher.
A. Babe Ruth
B. Lou Gehrig
C. Moises Alou
D. Willi Mays

402. Ryan Dempster's favorite type of food before a game?
A. Mexican
B. Italian
C. Chinese
D. French

403. Record for most at-bats is who?
A. Reggie Jackson
B. Ty Cobb
C. Hank Aaron
D. Pete Rose

404. Wore the name of his hometown on the back of his jersey?
A. Bill Voiselle
B. Joe Girardi
C. Willie Randolph
D. Willie Mays

"I won't be active in the day-to-day operations of the club at all."
George Steinbrenner, upon buying the Yankees in 1973.

405. Yogi Berra's real first name is what?
A. Sam
B. David
C. Lyle
D. Lawrence

406. Most career at-bats without a stolen base?
A. Ty Cobb
B. Don Kaiser
C. Hank Greenberg
D. Russ Nixon

407. Which is not a concession at any MLB ball park?
A. Burgerpizza
B. Toasted Grasshoppers
C. Monkey Brains
D. The Boomstick

408. Jason Giambi is known for what superstition?
A. Chicken Egg
B. Shoelaces
C. Seat Belt
D. Gold Thong

"Playing baseball for a living is like having a license to steal."
Pete Rose

409. Won Babe Ruth Award & Hutch Award & Lou Gehrig Award?
A. Johnny Bench
B. Roberto Clement
C. Willie Mays
D. Hank Aaron

410. How many "Private Luxury Suites" are there at Kauffmann Stadium?
A. 18
B. 24
C. 33
D. 48

411. Rickwood Field in Birmingham, Alabama was built in this year:
A. 1905
B. 1910
C. 1935
D. 1967

412. The most pickoffs recorded by a pitcher is 144 set by who?
A. Nolan Ryan
B. Greg Maddux
C. Cy Young
D. Steve Carlton

"The key to winning baseball games is pitching, fundamentals, and three-run homers."
Earl Weaver

413. What kind of grass is found in Marlins Park?

A. Bermuda
B. New-Age Synthetic Turf
C. St. Augustine
D. Bluegrass

414. Which player always threw out his gum before batting?

A. Willie Mays
B. Pete Rose
C. Lou Gehrig
D. Dick Stuart

415. His speech is considered the "Gettysburg Address of Baseball"?

A. Lou Gehrig
B. Babe Ruth
C. Pete Rose
D. Jackie Robinson

416. Tropicana Field is known for what?

A. Cotton Candy
B. Po' Boy Sandwich
C. Chili Fries
D. Cuban Sandwich

"People ask me what I do in winter when there's no baseball. I'll tell you what I do. I stare out the window and wait for spring."

Roger Hornsby

417. Who was known as "The Human Rain Delay" for at-bat routine?
A. Mike Hargrove
B. Hank Aaron
C. Babe Ruth
D. Barry Bonds

418. Who founded Los Angeles Angels in 1960?
A. Gene Autry
B. Bill Rigney
C. Del Rice
D. Bobby Winkles

419. He always touched the 2nd base when taking his position in center field?
A. Willie Mays
B. Joe DiMaggio
C. Ty Cobb
D. Duke Snider

420. This player had 120 intentional walks in 2004:
A. Barry Bonds
B. Bobby Abreu
C. Brian Giles
D. Dale Murphy

"If it wasn't for baseball, I'd either be in the penitentiary or the cemetery."
Babe Ruth

421. This player has a record of 7 MVP awards:
A. Barry Bonds
B. Hank Aaron
C. Cy Young
D. Sandy Koufax

422. This pitcher would wear a necklace made from hunted animal teeth:

A. Sandy Koufax
B. Cy Young
C. Turk Wendell
D. Randy Johnson

423. What is Matt Garza's favorite brand of chicken?
A. Church's
B. KFC
C. Zaxby's
D. Popeyes

424. This player holds the record for the most outs:
A. Pete Rose
B. Willie Mays
C. Babe Ruth
D. Lou Gehrig

"Baseball is the only field of endeavor where a man can succeed three times out of ten and be considered a good performer."
Ted Williams

425. He named one of his bats "Hrunting"?

A. Barry Bonds
B. Jackie Robinson
C. R.A. Dickey
D. Babe Ruth

426. The most at-bats in a career with no home runs?

A. Willie Holbert
B. Buddy Myer
C. Joe Vosmik
D. Bill Dailey

427. Who does the single red seat in Kauffman Stadium honor?

A. Jackie Robinson
B. Kyle Petty
C. Buck O' Neil
D. Michael Taylor

428. The youngest player as of 2020, to have ever won an MVP award.

A. Vida Blue
B. Opie Taylor
C. Luis Garcia
D. Charlie Eden

"Being with a woman all night never hurt no professional baseball player. It's staying up all night looking for a woman that does him in."
Casey Stengel

429. What are the team colors for the Atlanta Braves?
A. Deep Orange & Red
B. Black,Blue and Brown
C. Pink & Green
D. Navy Blue,Scarlet Red, and White

430. How many suites does Wrigley Field contain?
A. 21
B. 45
C. 64
D. 70

431. Had seven silver slugger awards and batting average of .338?
A. Tony Gwynn
B. Willie Mays
C. Barry Bonds
D. Ty Cobb

432. Which pitcher set a record for the most home runs allowed?
A. Cy Young
B. Roger Clemens
C. Nolan Ryan
D. Jamie Moyer

"There are three things you can do in a baseball game. You can win, or you can lose, or it can rain."
Casey Stengel

433. OF stands for what on scorecard?

A. Outfield
B. On Foul
C. Over Flanked
D. Over Free Base

434. Jackie Robinson played for which team?

A. New York Yankees
B. Atlanta Braves
C. Brooklyn Dodgers
D. Miami Marlins

435. This pitcher pitched a third and final no-hitter at age 44?
A. Greg Maddux
B. Babe Ruth
C. Nolan Ryan
D. John Smoltz

436. The mascot bear of the Twins is modeled after what?
A. Yogi
B. Smokey
C. Gentle Ben
D. Hamm's Beer Bear

"Doctors tell me I have the body of a thirty-year-old. I know I have the brain of a fifteen-year-old. If you've got both you can play baseball."
Pete Rose

437. Who would sleep with his bat before a game?
A. Ty Cobb
B. Hank Aaron
C. Reggie Jackson
D. Richie Ashburn

438. L stands for what on a scorecard.
A. Looser
B. Laughable
C. Link
D. Losses

439. He had a record career 309 Triples.
A. Sam Crawford
B. Stan Musial
C. Bobo Newsom
D. Hank Aaron

440. This player hit the only game 7 walk-off homer in World Series history?
A. Reggie Jackson
B. Hank Aaron
C. Ty Cobb
D. Bill Mazeroski

"I can remember a sportswriter asking me for a quote and I didn't know what a quote was. I thought it was some kind of soft drink."
Joe DiMaggio

441. He needed to pick up the ball from the ground before pitching.
A. John Smoltz
B. Greg Maddux
C. Don Robinson
D. Sandy Koufax

442. He ate same breakfast in order each game day?
A. Stan Musial
B. Pete Rose
C. Juan Samuel
D. Randy Johnson

443. Wore the same hat while on the mound pitching:
A. Tim Lincecum
B. Sandy Koufax
C. Greg Maddux
D. Nolan Ryan

444. This player went 57-48 as player-manager in only one season of the New York Yankees:
A. Bucky Dent
B. Bill Dickey
C. Billy Martin
D. Larry Rothschild

"The Yankees don't pay me to win every game-just two out of three."   Casey Stengel

445. Hit a grand slam from both sides of plate in same game in 2003:
A. Bill Mueller
B. Barry Bonds
C. Jim Thome
D. Carlos Delgado

446. Recognized as the original "Bernie Brewer"?
A. Milt Mason
B. Robin Yount
C. Jack Aker
D. Foster Brooks

447. Larry Doby played for which team?
A. Cleveland Indians
B. Baltimore Orioles
C. Pittsburgh Pirates
D. Atlanta Braves

448. The team that calls "Screech" their mascot is who?
A. Atlanta Braves
B. Boston Red Sox
C. Washington Nationals
D. New York Yankees

"I'm glad I don't play anymore. I could never learn all of those handshakes." Phil Rizzuto

449. Who would wear only one cap each season?

A. John Wetteland
B. Pete Rose
C. Ty Cobb
D. Hershel Walter

450. Who was hit more times with a pitch than any batter?

A. Craig Biggio
B. Hughie Jennings
C. Barry Bonds
D. Alan Shepard

451. This mascot was caught giving the middle finger to a fan in 2017:

A. Mariner Moose
B. Firebird
C. Mr. Met
D. Slugger

452. Who was the youngest player to "hit for the cycle"?

A. Mel Ott
B. Pete Rose
C. Ty Cobb
D. John Reilly

"They broke it to me gently. The manager came up to me before a game and told me they didn't allow visitors in the clubhouse."
Bob Uecker

453. When were the words written for Take Me Out To The Ball Game?
A. 1904
B. 1908
C. 1960
D. 1971

454. The "Clean Up Hitter" Burger can be found at this stadium:
A. Yankee Stadium
B. Fenway Park
C. Wrigley Field
D. Guaranteed Rate Field

455. Who insisted on new batting gloves after he made an out?
A. Lenny Dykstra
B. Rickey Henderson
C. George Brett
D. Willie Mays

456. This baseball card made a cameo appearance in "Home Alone":
A. Mickey Mantle
B. Bo Jackson
C. Fred McGriff
D. Babe Ruth

"He slides into second with a stand-up double."   Jerry Coleman

457. Enjoy a "Bacon Wrapped Hot Dog" at this ballpark:
A. Truist Park
B. Fenway Park
C. Busch Stadium
D. AT&T Park

458. Holds record for complete-game shutout with only 58 pitches:
A. Tom Seaver
B. Babe Ruth
C. Cy Young
D. Red Barrett

459. In 1999 this player hit two grand slams in the same inning:
A. Mark McGwire
B. Fernando Tatis
C. Derek Jeter
D. Sammy Sosa

460. What did not occur during years 1929-1952?
A. Gold Glove Awarded
B. Triple Play
C. World Series Shutout
D. Immaculate Inning

"I have an Alka-Seltzer bat. You know-plop, plop, fizz, fizz, when the pitcher sees me walking up there, he says, 'Oh, what a relief it is'."
Andy Van Slyke

461. Who won the first World Series in 1903?
A. Boston Americans
B. Miami Marlins
C. New York Yankees
D. Chicago Cubs

462. Pumpsie Green played for which team?
A. Atlanta Braves
B. New York Giants
C. Pittsburgh Pirates
D. Boston Red Sox

463. This player would keep four leaf clovers in his locker:
A. Pete Rose
B. Sherm Lollar
C. Ty Cobb
D. Homer Simpson

464. Youngest player to hit 100 home runs?
A. Mel Ott
B. Opie Taylor
C. Ty Cobb
D. Warren Spahn

"Why does everyone stand up and sing Take Me Out to the Ball Game when they're already there?"
Larry Anderson

465. Craig Biggio was known to cover his bat with what?

A. Owl Piss
B. WD 40
C. Pine Tar
D. Vaseline

466. In what year did Whitey Ford throw 283 innings without allowing a single steal?

A. 1955
B. 1958
C. 1961
D. 1971

467. This pitcher was known as a "Bonus Baby":

A. Sandy Koufax
B. Roger Clemens
C. Bob Gibson
D. Cy Young

468. You can find the "Pork Rind Chipper" at this ballpark:

A. Fenway Park
B. Yankee Stadium
C. Camden Yards
D. Truist Park

"I'm praying 2 things: Please God, don't let them hit it to me..and, please don't let them hit it to Steve Sax."
Pedro Guerrero

469. How many "Luxury Suites" does Yankee Stadium have?
A. 12
B. 26
C. 56
D. 70

470. You will find "Toasted Grasshoppers" served here:
A. Nationals Park
B. Great American Ball Park
C. Safeco Field
D. Yankee Stadium

471. Which pitcher has the lowest E.R.A. at 1.82?
A. Ed Walsh
B. Roger Clemens
C. Nolan Ryan
D. Babe Ruth

472. What does the acronym IP stand for?
A. Initial Pitcher
B. In a Pinch
C. Innings Pitched
D. Inside Pitch

"They should move back first base a step to eliminate all those close plays."
John Lowenstein

473. He hit a grand slam on the first pitch he saw in big leagues:
A. Pete Rose
B. Hank Aaron
C. Lou Gehrig
D. Kevin Kouzmanoff

474. Fredbird is what type of bird?
A. Swann
B. Crow
C. Cardinal
D. Eagle

475. The number of shutouts that both Tom Seaver & Nolan Ryan tied for.
A. 40
B. 49
C. 507
D. 61

476. Wore #10 and was inducted to Hall of Fame his first year of eligibility:
A. Michael Young
B. Chipper Jones
C. Tom Kelly
D. Sparky Anderson

"They give you a round bat and they throw you a round ball. And they tell you to hit it square."
Willie Stargell

477. Who holds record for most RBIs?
A. Tom Seaver
B. Ty Cobb
C. Joe DiMaggio
D. Hank Aaron

478. The only stadium that sells more sausages than hot dogs:
A. Dodger Stadium
B. Fenway Park
C. Petco Field
D. Miller Park

479. What is the most popular type of grass used on MLB fields?
A. St. Augustine
B. Kentucky Bluegrass
C. Zosia
D. Bahia Grass

480. He decided to wear two mismatched socks:
A. Pete Rose
B. Ty Cobb
C. Mark Teixeira
D. Hank Aaron

"I never questioned the integrity of an umpire. Their eyesight, yes."
Leo Durocher

481. This player was thrown out 4 times trying to steal in one game in 1986:
A. Harry Bay
B. Frank Isbell
C. Robby Thompson
D. Lyn Lary

482. He pitched consecutive no-hitters four days apart in 1938:
A. Bob Feller
B. BoBo Newsom
C. Lefty Grove
D. Johnny Vander Meer

483. What year did Ted Williams retire?
A. 1945
B. 1955
C. 1960
D. 1971

484. Who was the youngest player to make a MLB debut in 1944?
A. Joe Nuxhall
B. Bryce Harper
C. Jamie Moyers
D. Jackie Robinson

"If you don't think too good, don't think too much."

Ted Williams

485. David Ortiz always spit on what before an at-bat?
A. His Bat
B. Home Plate
C. Catcher
D. Batting Glove

486. What does the acronym ER stand for?

A. Early Release
B. Error Rounding Base
C. Earned Runs
D. Etched Runner

487. Who is not a pitcher in this set of names?
A. Sandy Koufax
B. Bob Gibson
C. Hank Aaron
D. Roger Clemens

488. Holds record for most times caught stealing bases (335):
A. Rickey Henderson
B. Pete Rose
C. Ty Cobb
D. Jose Offerman

"I don't want to play golf. When I hit a ball, I want others to chase it."

Rogers Hornsby

489. What does HRR stand for?
A. High Ratio Runner
B. Hit Runner Revenge
C. Home Run Ratio
D. High Relief Ranked

490. Come to Dodger Stadium to enjoy what?
A. Fudge Brownie & Jell-O
B. Tuna on Rye
C. Super Dodger Dog
D. Spaghetti and Meatballs

491. Not featured on any mainstream baseball cards from 1954-1957:
A. Sandy Koufax
B. Stan Musial
C. Bob Lemon
D. Robin Roberts

492. World Series first to have a game scheduled at night:
A. 1971
B. 1973
C. 1980
D. 1985

"All ballplayers should quit when it starts to feel as if all the baselines run uphill."
Babe Ruth

493. How many total suites does Fenway Park have?
A. 20
B. 30
C. 52
D. 112

494. Which pitcher holds the record for most losses?
A. Tom Seaver
B. Randy Johnson
C. Sandy Koufax
D. Cy Young

495. What is the Boston Red Sox' team colors?
A. Green & Midnight Blue
B. Cherry Red & Mustard Yellow
C. Red Hot & Blue Night
D. Red, Navy Blue and White

496. In 1912 this ballpark was completed:
A. Yankee Stadium
B. Truist Park
C. Safeco Field
D. Fenway Park

"It ain't nothing till I call it."
Bill Klem, former MLB umpire

497. Monte Irvin played for which team?

A. New York Yankees
B. Brooklyn Dodgers
C. Houston Astros
D. New York Giants

498. SB stands for what?

A. Sad Balls
B. Sick Backup
C. Stolen Base
D. Stuck Ball

499. Who won Rookie of the Year in 2012 unanimously?

A. Mike Trout
B. Todd Frazier
C. Jordan Pacheco
D. Yu Darvish

500. Baseball field lines are made with what material?
A. Borax
B. Baby Powder
C. Limestone
D. Flour

Answers 1-500

The Baseball Addicts Trivia Book

Copyright 2021
Chip Trellix
Trellix Trivia Publishing

1. How many players make up the roster of an MLB team?

26

2. Another name for the baseball manager is what?

Skipper

3. You can enjoy nachos in a replica helmet at this park:

Angel Stadium

4. A manager is known to apply the hook when he changes what?

Pitchers

5. First player to claim 17 MLB Triple Crowns in 45 seasons is who?

Miguel Cabrera

6. At 3 feet 7inches who was shortest player to bat in a MLB game?

Eddie Gaedel

7. Sandy Koufax pitched for the Brooklyn/L.A. Dodgers:

Twelve Seasons

8. He was recruited by MLB ,the NFL, and the NBA, who was he?

Dave Winfield

9. How fast does a ball bat travel in a swing?

80mph

10. A moon shot represents what?

High Home Run

11. How many balls do you need to get a walk?

4

12. Appeared in 3 straight World Series with 3 different teams?

Don Baylor

13. 3 and 2 is known as a what?

Full Count

14. A pitch that almost hits the batter is known as a what?

Brushback

15. According to John Fogerty -"Look at me, I can be_____"?

Center Field

16. How many Division Titles have the New York Yankees won?

19

17. Traded by L.A. Dodgers for being too small as a pitcher?

Pedro Martinez

18. A Ground into Double Play is what abbreviation?

GIDP

19. In 2004 this player reached base three times more than at-bat?

Barry Bonds

20. Since 2020 team has gone longest without winning World Series?

Seattle Mariners

21. Base coaches help who?

Base Runners

22. Good Humor Fan Fest is found in which stadium?

Citi Field

23. About how many baseballs do all 30 MLB teams use per season together?

918000

24. Hank Aaron played for who when he beat Babe Ruth's record?

Atlanta Braves

25. How many Gold Glove awards did Hank Aaron win in his career?

3

26. Another term for a hit is what?

Knock

27. Who was the winningest pitcher in the 1960s with 191 wins?

Juan Marichal

28. Fastest inside-the-park home run was by who at 14.29 sec in 2014?

Kevin Kiermaier

29. The first left-hander member of the 300 Win Club?

Eddie Plank

30. Who's 1994 start was pushed back for tattoo infection?

Jeff Juden

31. A team not doing well is considered in a what?

Slump

32. First player who had their number retired by all MLB teams:

Jackie Robinson

33. Bo Jackson's #697 ball card was in what company's Ad campaign?

Nike

34. First U.S. President to throw the ceremonial first ball:

William Howard Taft

35. A changeup is what?

Type of Pitch

36. Charlie Hustle was the nickname for which player?

Pete Rose

37. A pitcher that throws with a severe sidearm motion is known as a what?

Submarine Pitcher

38. Which player was given a World War I draft deferment to support family?

Rogers Hornsby

39. A ball hit on the ground producing an out?

Groundout

40. First base runner when bases are loaded is known as a what?

Lead Runner

41. Who was the first player to wear sunglasses?

Paul Hines

42. A home run hit with no runners already on base:

Solo Home Run

43. How many teams did Jim Thome play for 1991 to 2012?

Six

44. First year Topps used unaltered photos for their base set:

1957

45. This pitcher struck out five hitters in 1934 All-Star game with screwball:

Curt Davis

46. Which pitcher did not have a right hand?

Jim Abbott

47. How many baseballs are used in a typical MLB game?

120

48. How many MLB players have hit 3 home runs on Opening Day?

4

49. Accounted for nearly half of Phillies wins as pitcher in 1972?

Steve Carlton

50. He recorded a hit for two teams in two cities on the same day?

Joel Youngblood

51. A tater is another word for what?

Home Run

52. Batting average is noted as this abbreviation on a scorecard?

AVG

53. The penalty for a balk is known as a what ?

Dead Ball

54. How many baseballs could Johnny Bench hold in one hand?

7

55. 2B is known as what on scorecards?

Double

56. Grover Cleveland Alexander elected to Hall of Fame in what year?

1938

57. A baseball game usually lasts for how many hours?

3 Hours

58. How many games did Wade Boggs reach base safely in 1985?

152

59. Extra innings are known as what?

Free Baseball

60. First player to score a hit in the newly formed National League:

Jim O'Rourke

61. How many baseball games are in a season?

162

62. A substitute base runner is known as what?

Pinch Runner

63. Baseball was invented in the 1800s with which rules?

 Knickerbocker

64. A batter known to hit line drives everywhere is a what?

Spray Hitter

65. The Houston Astros and their fans celebrate their history at this place:

Home Run Alley

66. How many decades did Nolan Ryan's career span?

Four

67. Players achieving "natural cycles" in "at bat" during a game? 13

68. What is Joe DiMaggio's hometown?

Matinez, CA

69. AB is known as what on a scorecard?

At-bat

70. A hitter that pulls to the side he is hitting:

Pull Hitter

71. First umpire to use instant replay to reverse a call:

Frank Pulli

72. Area that consists of the grass beyond infield is known as what?

Outfield

73. How is sac fly abbreviated on a scorecard?

SF

74. A player that never won MVP but stole over 800 bases is who?

Tim Raines

75. Who was the first to sign a contract worth one million dollars per season? Nolan Ryan

76. He was a lifetime Kansas City Royal for 21 years?

George Brett

77. A pickle is known as what?

A Rundown

78. Fenway Park is known for its what?

Autograph Alley

79. How many no-hitters were thrown in the 2012 regular season?

 7

80. CS stands for what on a scorecard?

Caught Stealing

81. Another word for an easily handled pitch is what?

Salad

82. How many pitchers have recorded over 600 complete games?

Two

83. Coaches use what to hit to infielders during practice?

Fungo Bats

84. A curve ball is also known as what?

Uncle Charlie

85. A strong long-distance hitter is known as a what?

Power Hitter

86. Who is the first fielder to throw out three runners at home plate?

Jack McCarthy (4-26-1905)

87. Cy Young Award was first awarded in what year?

1956

88. Who holds the record for stealing home plate?

Ty Cobb

89. Metal-halides are used for what in baseball stadiums?

Light Stadium

90. Who won 3 Cy Young awards in his career?

Jim Palmer

91. Baseball is played on a geometrical shaped field known as a what?

Diamond

92. A pitcher that pitches an entire game is known to have a what?

Complete Game

93. Dodger Stadium opened in what year?

1962

94. Prior to 2013, who was the grand slam leader?

Lou Gehrig

95. A ball hit back to the pitcher is what?

Comebacker

96. An organic restaurant can be found in this park? AT&T Park

97. Which player won a World Series MVP for a losing team?

Bobby Richardson

98. Hank Aaron grew up in what city?

Mobile

99. A splitter is a type of what?

Pitch

100. Games played is represented by what abbreviation on scorecards? G

101. The Baker Bowl was once known as what?

National League Park

102. What player missed a start by getting bitten by his mother-in-law's dog.

David Cone

103. The fastest baseball pitch recorded for a woman was what?

69mph

104. The Bullpen Market can be found here:

Safeco Field

105. Building of Baseball Hall of Fame was built in what year?

1939

106. Interact with this friend at Tropicana Field center field:

Stingray

107. Who wore his entire birthday of May 17 on back of uniform?

Carlos May

108. The Gold Glove Award was first awarded in what year?

1957

109. Which pitcher holds the all-time Major League record for home runs hit while playing the position of pitcher?

Wes Ferrell

110. The Green Monster is in which ballpark?

Fenway Park

111. The 1927 Yankee lineup was known as what?

Murderer's Row

112. Stadium with "Federal Donuts" for concessions:

Citizens Bank Park

113. All-Star games played record by Hank Aaron was how many?

25

114. Who won the MVP in both American and National Leagues?

Frank Robinson

115. Mickey Mantle's nickname was what?

The Mick

116. If a batter commits a whiff, they have what?

Struck Out

117. Only pitcher in history to throw no-hitter on his birthday.

George Mullen

118. No RBI was awarded in this year's All-Star game:

1968

119. Ride a Carousel at this ballpark:

Comerica Park

120. Most popular ballpark food is what?

Hot Dogs

121. The most innings pitched in a season was pitched by who?
Will White

122. Hit forty home runs & hit .400 or better in single season?
Rogers Hornsby

123. In 1962 which pitcher struck out the first six batters he faced?
Pete Richert

124. If runners are on second and third bases, they are in what?
Scoring Position

125. Small theatre provides history of Kansas City Royals where?
Kauffman Stadium

126. Ozzie Smith was known as what?
The Wizard of Oz

127. Who was the last pitcher to legally throw a spitball?
Burleigh Grimes

128. Who is the record holder for the most RBIs in a season?
Hack Wilson

129. Who struck out Ruth and Gehrig in succession & banned from MLB?
Jackie Mitchell

130. The quickest game in MLB took place Oct 28, 1919 and lasted how long?
51 Minutes

131. The most career shutouts by a pitcher is who?
Walter Johnson

132. The phrase "walk-off homerun" did not apply before this year?
1988, coined by Dennis Eckersley

133. Rod Carew was named All-Star how many times?
Eighteen

134. The first and only 500 game winner is which pitcher?
Cy Young

135. 1st card to show - "saves as a pitcher"- stat made by who?
Donruss

136. The name for baseball fans in the early days?
Cranks

137. Pitch delivered after a full count?

Payoff Pitch

138. Who was the oldest to hit a home run at 47 years 240 days old?

Julio Franco

139. In 2004 this player reached base more times than at-bat:

Barry Bonds

140. How many times did Babe Ruth reach base safely in 1923?

379

141. What year did the L.A. Angels begin to play in the MLB, as a new expansion to the American League?

1961

142. The COP is also known as what?

Sweet Spot

143. A great stadium with something located in center field for fans:

Yankee Stadium

144. The most All-Star games played by Hank Aaron was how many?

25

145. The record for most road losses in a season are 101 by this team:

Cleveland Spiders

146. Who holds the record for most assists in a single season?

Orator Shafer

147. What was the number of hits recorded by MLB record holder Pete Rose?

4256

148. If you win the league championship you win what?

The Pennant

149. The most expensive autographed baseball sold for how much?

$632,369 (Signed by 11 baseball early greats)

150. In baseball a fight that breaks out is known as a what?

Rhubarb

151. Most hits in a season as of 2004 was by who?
Ichiro Suzuki

152. Player was struck by Lightning in 1914 while catching fly ball?

Red Murray

153. The last major park to install lights was which stadium?

Wrigley Field

154. Who is the only pitcher to pitch to a horse on a TV show in 1963?

Sandy Koufax

155. Monument Park is to Yankee fans as Heritage Park is to?

Indian Fans

156. How many stitches make up a major league baseball?

108

157. Player with most career MLB hits?

Pete Rose

158. Johnny Bench played what position for the Cincinnati Reds?

Catcher

159. Set record for most career complete games?

Cy Young

160. One of the best left-handed pitchers in history was who?

Lefty Grove

161. Rickwood Field is located where?

Birmingham

162. The only player killed by a major league pitch by Carl Mays?

Ray Chapman

163. People knew Joe DiMaggio as what?

Joltin' Joe

164. Who was known as Mr. October ?

Reggie Jackson

165. What was Hank Aaron's nickname ?

Hammerin' Hank

166. The "Hill" is what?

Pitcher's Mound

167. John Smoltz's age when returning to rotation after injury?

39

168. 7 Fountains erupt at this stadium when the home team hits a homerun:

Coors Field

169. How much did Mark McGwire's 70th home run baseball sell for?

Three Million

170. Longest hitting streak was 56 games set in 1941 by who?

Joe DiMaggio

171. How many times did Topps feature Tommy Davis on a different team from 1966-1972 ?

Seven

172. PB stands for what on scorecard?

Passed Ball

173. "How many teams did Rusty Staub have 500 hits with?

Four

174. Natural frequency of a wooden bat is what?

250 Hertz

175. Record holder for consecutive no-hitters:

Johnny Vander Meer

176. Longest baseball game in history lasted how many innings?

25

177. Miami Marlins Park has a nightclub named what?

The Clevelander

178. Which catcher holds the record catching for 25 innings?

Carlton Fisk

179. Who is the only pitcher to strike out Tony Gwynn three times in a game?

Bob Welch

180. Most career wild pitches thrown was by who?

Tony Mullane

181. HP stands for what on scorecard?

Hit by pitch

182. The first World Series took place in what year?

1903

183. The highest level of seats in a stadium?

Nosebleed Seats

184. The only player to have worn all 4 of the New York franchises' uniforms:

Casey Stengel

185. The most career sacrifice bunts record holder for the US Major League is who?

Eddie Collins

186. How many times did Nolan Ryan strike out 163 different batters?

Ten

187. Only player to hit the warehouse behind Camden Yards:

Ken Griffey Jr.

188. What stadium did Pope John Paul II lead mass in 1987:

Dodger Stadium

189. Who is the record holder for most career no-hitters?

Nolan Ryan

190. The San Diego Padres stadium is known as what?

Petco Park

191. Larry "Chipper" Jones is best known for what position?

Third Baseman

192. How many sides does Home Plate have?

Five

193. Rule 7.08i denotes what?

Putting Out a Base Runner

194. Who is the only pitcher in majors to record both 200 wins and 150 saves?

John Smoltz

195. The batting order of players is also known as what ?

Lineup

196. Jimmy Piersall suffered from what?

Bipolar Disorder

197. "When did both the New York Giants and Philadelphia Phillies pitch the idea of wearing pinstripes?

"1911 Giants began wearing them that year but Phillies began to wear them in 1921.

198. The ballpark with fire pits is known as what ball field?

Target Field

199. Manny's is known for what type of food at PNC Park in Pittsburg?

Pulled Pork BBQ

200. How many teams make up the playoffs?

Ten

201. The Beatles played their first U.S. summer tour concert here:
Shea Stadium

202. Had a statue erected of himself in his backyard:
Ivan Rodriguez

203. The worst injury that a pitcher can have is a what?
Labrum Tear

204. Number worn by Sandy Koufax & Elston Howard in 1963 MVP Awards? 32

205. This pitcher's wife filed for divorce before his perfect 1956 World Series Game?
Don Larsen

206. The abbreviation BK is used for what on scorecards?
Balk

207. Which of these is not a type of pitch?
Snotball

208. Jim Hunter's nickname was which of these fish?
Catfish

209. This pitcher won a game with only one pitch:

Ken Ash

210. He threw out three runners at home plate in the same inning:

Jack McCarthy

211. He hit the longest home run ever hit in San Francisco:

Willie McCovey

212. When a batter is called out on strikes, he is what?

Caught Looking

213. Pitched perfect game in World Series history in 1956?

Don Larsen

214. The Rubber Game in a series is known as what?

Deciding Game

215. The Texas Rangers formed, and was known as the Washington Senators and known as Washington Senators in what year?

1961

216. The first year that a sitting president attended a World Series game.

1915

217. Banned from baseball for betting on games while managing team:
Pete Rose

218. Who was enshrined in the Baseball Hall of Fame in its first class?
Christy Mathewson

219. What is a pitched ball that travels at high speed called ?
Pea

220. What position did Josh Gibson play?
Catcher

221. Which team wore the first baseball uniforms ?
Knickerbockers

222. What is a one base hit known as?
Single

223. Only 2 positions that allowed or required to use a Mitt?
Catcher & First Base

224. This pitcher's fastball was clocked at 102 mph.
Randy Johnson

225. Where is the Keystone Sack located on a baseball diamond?

Second Base

226. Who was a fourteen time All-Star and won a Gold Glove?

Ernie Banks

227. What year was a game called in New York in the sixth inning due to snowball fights amongst fans?

1907

228. Which inning is the Baseball Anthem played at every MLB game?

Seventh

229. Which Mickey was nicknamed "Black Mike"?

Mickey Cochrane

230. What disease forced Lou Gehrig to retire?

Amyotrophic Lateral Sclerosis

231. Which manager was ejected from a record 91 games?

Earl Weaver

232. What Character was inspired by Yogi Berra?

Yogi Bear

233. This player had seven straight seasons with at least 200 hits: Wade Boggs

234. What ball field was built on land owned by Babe Ruth's father's saloon?

Camden Yards

235. How many consecutive games from 1982 to 1998 did Cal Ripken Jr. play in?

2,632

236. What is the oldest MLB ballpark?

Fenway Park

237. Who was the owner that wanted Day-Glo orange baseballs used?

Charles O. Finley

238. What is "Billie the Marlin?"

A Fish

239. What number did Babe Ruth wear?

3

240. Had a voting percentage of (98.5%) in the Hall of Fame in 2007? Cal Ripken Jr.

241. Pitcher with 363 wins (6th most in MLB) & lifetime ERA of 3.09?

Warren Spahn

242. He died the same day as actor Christopher Reeve.

Ken Caminiti

243. "The Rocket" was a nickname for this player:

Roger Clemens

244. What is the area between the foul lines, and including the foul poles called?

Fair Territory

245. Which player injured himself with his own false teeth?

Clarence Blethen

246. What position did Lou Gehrig play?

First Base

247. Which company produced the Frank Thomas "No Name on Front" #414 baseball card?

Topps

248. Joel Zumaya once missed three games in 2006 doing what?

Playing Guitar Hero

249. Ty Cobb was known as what?

The Georgia Peach

250. What is the max numerical slugging percentage, even though no player has ever recorded this feat?

Four Thousand

251. Which player gave up three years of career to fight in WWII?

Hank Greenberg

252. What year were wax pack cards offered by the Topps baseball card company?
1952

253. Which is considered a hot corner on a baseball field?

Third Base

254. Where did Jackie Robinson play his first MLB game?

Ebbets Field

255. Which position wears the "Tools of Ignorance"?

Catcher

256. What do the Hall of Fame members Bob Gibson, Lou Brock and Fergie Jenkins have in common?

They all played for the Harlem Globetrotters

257. Who was the first player in NL history to hit 2 grand slams in 1 game?

Tony Cloninger

258. Which pitcher faced Roger Maris, Mark McGwire, and Barry Bonds? Nolan Ryan

259. This type of pitch nearly hits the batter:

Brushback

260. What year was Frankie Frisch voted into the Hall of Fame?

1947

261. Tom Seaver won the World Series in 1969 with which team?

New York Mets

262. Which city has oldest baseball stadium still in use by the MLB?

Boston

263. Which base is considered the most stolen base in MLB?

Second Base

264. What do batters use to increase a bat's weight during practice?

Donut

265. How did the Brooklyn Dodgers get their name?

Dodging Trolley Cars

266. When was Frankie Frisch voted into the Baseball Hall of Fame?

1947

267. Which former Pro football player became an AL MLB umpire in 1936?

Cal Hubbard

268. What year was the wild card rule introduced to baseball?

1994

269. Which company sponsors Gold Glove Award?

Rawlings

270. Two or three players on base are known as what?

Ducks on the Pond

271. Which of the following will bat second and play at their stadium?

Home Team

272. Distance between bases on a typical MLB baseball field?

90 feet

273. Which pitcher made 24 quality starts out of 25 games in 1994?

Greg Maddux

274. Tom Seaver was also known as what?

Tom Terrific

275. This ballpark is home to a famous beer:

Miller Park

276. This player died in a tragic plane crash who was he?

Roberto Clemente

277. Barrelman belongs to which team?

Milwaukee Brewers

278. This team managed to turn two triple plays in 1990 into loss:

Minnesota Twins

279. What year did two deaf players face each other in a game?

1902

280. Which of these pitchers did not play in the 1980s?

Cy Young

281. The third base umpire position is known as what?

Rocking Chair

282. Which baseball glove company did not originate in the USA?

Mizuno

283. What's the most valuable baseball card in the world?

1909 T206 Honus Wagner

284. Number Derek Jeter wore and retired in 2017 by New York Yankees?

#2

285. What is the player after the on-deck player called?

In the Hole

286. In the 1977 World Series, what player hit 3 home runs in a row at Yankee Stadium?

Reggie Jackson

287. Opening day 2018 for the Atlanta Braves produced which mascot?

Blooper

288. The record of 29 postseason home runs belongs to whom?

Manny Ramirez

289. Who was the youngest inductee elected to the Hall of Fame in 1972, at the age of 36?

Sandy Koufax

290. The Second Baseman is what number in the scorebook?

4

291. Which baseball card was featured in the movie "The Accountant?"

T206 Honus Wagner

292. Record for most often hit by a pitch is who?

Hughie Jenning

293. Baxter the Bobcat belongs to which team?

Arizona Diamondbacks

294. What number is the right fielder on a scorecard?

9

295. What is it sometimes called when a batter makes ideal contact with the ball?

On the Screws

296. Which base is known as the dish?

Home Plate

297. Which player missed his start in 2001 because he stabbed himself while opening a package?

Adam Eaton

298. Secret location a baseball gets a mud rubdown before use?

New Jersey

299. Which player ran the bases backward to celebrate his 100th home run?

Jimmy Piersall

300. What is the name of the Toronto Blue Jays mascot?

Ace

301. Who set record for most career triples?

Sam Crawford

302. Mickey Mantle was what number?

7

303. Another name for a fastball is what?

Cheese

304. Who was first deaf baseball player?

William Hoy

305. Called last game as home-plate umpire in "56" World Series:

Babe Pinelli

306. Who had 45 career four-hit games?

Tony Gwynn

307. What is an "Ace"?

Starting Pitcher

308. What is a beanball known as?

Pitch that Hits Batter in Head

309. The first domed stadium in the world was what?

Astrodome

310. Who holds record for most All-Star selections at a total of 25?

Hank Aaron

311. Only player appearing with mustache in Topps T206 set of cards?

John Titus

312. What number is associated with Derek Jeter?

2

313. Who was named as MVP in the 1999 World Series?

Mariano Rivera

314. Who was the only player to play for same team in 3 different cities?

Eddie Mathews

315. Who was an All-Star nine times in his career?

Jimmie Foxx

316. Hit only home run 20 min after Neil Armstrong walked on moon.

Gaylord perry

317. 14-time All-Star winner and suspended twice for steroids use?

Alex Rodriguez

318. What number did Wade Boggs wear for Boston?

26

319. Who is the first player to use a helmet?

Buster Mills

320. "Rookie of the Year" first time award was given:

Jackie Robinson

321. Who set the record for most RBIs (40) in World Series play?

Mickey Mantle

322. What Position did Joe Morgan play?

2nd Baseman

323. Who is the first left-hander member of the 300 Win Club?

Eddie Plank

324. This team outhit Cleveland in 1920 series but still lost (8-1):

Brooklyn Dodgers

325. Who is record holder for consecutive no-hitters?

Johnny Vander Meer

326. What does DP stand for?

Double Play

327. Who was walked more times than any other player?

Barry Bonds

328. What does "Around the Horn" refer to?

Triple Play

329. Outfielder Mookie Betts of the Sox was fearful of what?

Rust

330. Who was the major league's oldest rookie?

Satchel Paige

331. What does "RISP" stand for?

Runners in Scoring Position

332. Who was the only sportswriter elected to Baseball Hall of Fame?

Henry Chadwick

333. The mascot "Paws" likes to hang out with which team?
Detroit Tigers

334. Who is the first pitcher to win 3 or more Cy Young Awards?

Steve Carlton

335. Who threw first no-hitter in Coors Field?

Hideo Nomo

336. One of 29 players to appear in MLB games in 4 calendar decades.

Ken Griffey Jr.

337. Hit 53 of the 212 home runs in 2013 for Orioles?

Chris Davis

338. Who struck out 26% of batters he faced in the 1970s?

Nolan Ryan

339. What position did Reggie Jackson play?

Right Fielder

340. The first mascot to exist in human form was what?

Mr. Met

341. Who stole 138 bases in 1887?

Hugh Nicol

342. Who was banned for life from Baseball Hall of Fame?

Pete Rose

343. Who was the first player to hit 54 home runs in one season?

Babe Ruth

344. This Cleveland mascot celebrated its 29th birthday July 29th of 2019:

Slider

345. Who played in 3 straight World Series for 3 different teams?

Don Baylor

346. Who holds record for most triples in a lifetime?

Sam Crawford

347. Rafael Palmeiro tested positive for drugs when?

2005

348. Who was the first woman to do play-by-play for White Sox?

Mary Shane

349. Who was the Dodger announcer when Hank Aaron hit record home run?

Vin Scully

350. Who struck out both Bobby Bonds and Barry Bonds?

Nolan Ryan

351. Who is known to "shut the door" if their team wins?

Closing Pitcher

352. What are the main colors of the Baltimore Orioles Mascot?

Orange & Black

353. Which team was the first to introduce Salaries for its players?

Cincinnati Red Stockings

354. What number does Ozzie Smith wear?

1

355. Who was inducted to Hall of Fame as a second baseman in 1990?

Joe Morgan

356. Which left-handed left-handed pitcher had second-most lifetime strikeouts?

Steve Carlton

357. Who played 2632 games straight?

Cal Ripken JR.

358. One of the best pitching rotations in history in the 1990s? Atlanta Braves

359. Who said, "We made too many wrong mistakes?"

Yogi Berra

360. Earned Runs is abbreviated as what?

ER

361. Who was the first National League player to hit 500 home runs?

Mel Ott

362. First African American pitcher in World Series game?

Satchel Paige

363. First A. L. pitcher with 2 complete Game victories in 1 day?

Frank Owen

364. First to wear numbers on the back of their jerseys?

Cleveland Indians

365. What year did Hank Aaron appear on a Wheaties box?

2002

366. Another word for home run is what?

Dinger

367. Who was part of Yankees dynasty that won 5 Straight World series?Johnny Mize

368. Which player played 3 different positions and was 7 times All-Star?

Craig Biggio

369. First World Series to have a game scheduled at night?

1971

370. Who had a single season (1924) record batting average of .424?

Rogers Hornsby

371. Who was 10x Silver Slugger and Hall of Famer Catcher?

 Mike Piazza

372. Who was an eight-time All-Star pitcher for Cleveland Indians?

Bob Feller

373. Orbit belongs to which team?

Houston Astros

374. First baseball player to appear on a Wheaties cereal box (1934):

Lou Gehrig

375. Bag is another word for what?

Base

376. What number did Tom Seaver wear for the Mets?

41

377. Who coined the term "sabermetrics"?

Bill James

378. Which World Series was never actually played?

Second

379. Found not guilty of lying to congress on all 6 counts in 2012?

Roger Clemens

380. Who had ten career steals of home plate?

Babe Ruth

381. Which team had 4 thirty home run hitters in the same season?

Los Angeles Dodgers

382. Who played for Cincinnati Reds from 1967 to 1983 as catcher?

Johnny Bench

383. Won a silver medal as a speed skater in 2014 Winter Olympics?

Eddy Alvarez

384. What type of mascot is "Captain", the mascot of the Texas Rangers?

Horse

385. What does CS stand for?

Caught Stealing

386. Who had Nine All-Star Awards and Eight Silver Slugger Awards?

Vladimir Guerrero

387. When a batter hits a ball between 2 outfielders it is a what?

Gapper

388. The first home run by a pitcher in World Series happened when?

1920

389. Who was a 2-time World Series winner and 2 times CY Young Award?

Bob Gibson

390. Who is the first member of the 3000 hit Club?

Cap Anson

391. Which pitcher said he threw his June 12, 1970 no-hitter under the influence of LSD?

Doc Ellis

392. As many career wins as hits in career that included 363?

Warren Spahn

393. Who had his number 42 retired by every team in baseball in 1992?
Jackie Robinson

394. Who was nicknamed Mr. October?
Reggie Jackson

395. Who was the first athlete of any sport to be on the cover of Sports Illustrated?
Eddie Mathews

396. Who hit a homerun into a Tuba?
Willie Stargell

397. Which player had the highest career batting average of .366?
Ty Cobb

398. What do both Lance Armstrong & Alex Rodriguez share in common?Both Failed Drug Test

399. Stomper would be at home where?
RingCentral Coliseum

400. Which name is not an actual name of any MLB player?
Snarrelgasinski

401. Which player was known for peeing on his hands to make them tougher.

Moises Alou

402. Ryan Dempster's favorite type of food before a game?

Italian

403. Record for most at-bats is who?

Pete Rose

404. Wore the name of his hometown on the back of his jersey?

Bill Voiselle

405. Yogi Berra's real first name is what?

Lawrence

406. Most career at-bats without a stolen base?

Russ Nixon

407. Which is not a concession at any MLB ball park?

Monkey Brains

408. Jason Giambi is known for what superstition?

Gold Thong

409. Won Babe Ruth Award & Hutch Award & Lou Gehrig Award?

Johnny Bench

410. How many "Private Luxury Suites" are there at Kauffmann Stadium?

33

411. Rickwood Field in Birmingham, Alabama was built in this year:

1910

412. Most pickoffs recorded by a pitcher is 144 set by who?

Steve Carlton

413. What kind of grass is found in Marlins Park?

new-age synthetic turf

414. Which player always threw out his gum before batting?

Dick Stuart

415. His speech is considered the "Gettysburg Address of Baseball"?

Lou Gehrig

416. Tropicana Field is known for what?

Cuban Sandwich

417. Who was known as "The Human Rain Delay" for at-bat routine?

Mike Hargrove

418. Who founded Los Angeles Angels in 1960?

Gene Autry

419. He always touched 2nd base when taking position in center field?

Joe DiMaggio

420. This player had 120 intentional walks in 2004:

Barry Bonds

421. This player has a record of 7 MVP awards:

Barry Bonds

422. This pitcher would wear a necklace made from hunted animal teeth:

Turk Wendell

423. What is Matt Garza's favorite brand of chicken?

Popeyes

424. This player holds the record for the most outs:

Pete Rose

425. He named one of his bats "Hrunting"?

R.A. Dickey

426. Most at-bats in a career with no home runs?

Willie Holbert

427. Who does the single red seat in Kauffman Stadium honor?

Buck O' Neil

428. Youngest player as of 2020 to have ever won MVP award.

Vida Blue

429. What are the team colors for the Atlanta Braves?

Navy Blue, Scarlet Red, and White

430. How many suites does Wrigley Field contain?

70

431. Had seven silver slugger awards and batting average of .338:

Tony Gwynn

432. Which pitcher set a record for most home runs allowed?

Jamie Moyer

433. OF stands for what on scorecard?

Outfield

434. Jackie Robinson played for which team?

Brooklyn Dodgers

435. This pitcher pitched a third and final no-hitter at age 44:

Nolan Ryan

436. The mascot bear of the Twins is modeled after what?

Hamm's Beer Bear

437. Who would sleep with his bat before a game?

Richie Ashburn

438. L stands for what on a scorecard.

Losses

439. He had a record career 309 Triples.

Sam Crawford

440. Hit the only game 7 walk-off homer in World Series history:

Bill Mazeroski

441. He needed to pick up ball from ground before pitching.

Don Robinson

442. Who ate the same breakfast in the same order every game day?

Stan Musial

443. Wore the same hat while on the mound pitching:

Tim Lincecum

444. This player went 57-48 as player-manager in only one season of the New York Yankees:

Bill Dickey

445. Hit a grand slam from both sides of plate in same game in 2003:

Bill Mueller

446. Recognized as the original "Bernie Brewer"?

Milt Mason

447. Larry Doby played for which team?

Cleveland Indians

448. The team that calls "Screech" their mascot is who?

Washington Nationals

449. Who would wear only one cap each season?

John Wetteland

450. Who was hit more times with a pitch than any batter?

Hughie Jennings

451. This mascot was caught giving the middle finger in 2017:

Mr. Met

452. Who was the youngest player to "hit for the cycle"?

Mel Ott

453. When were the words written for Take Me Out to the Ball Game?

1904

454. The "Clean Up Hitter" Burger can be found at this stadium:

Guaranteed Rate Field

455. Who insisted on new batting gloves after he made an out?

Lenny Dykstra

456. Baseball card made a cameo appearance in "Home Alone":

Fred McGriff

457. Enjoy a "Bacon Wrapped Hot Dog" at this ballpark:

Busch Stadium

458. Holds record for complete-game shutout with only 58 pitches:

Red Barrett

459. In 1999 this player hit two grand slams in the same inning:

Fernando Tatis

460. What did not occur during years 1929-1952?

Immaculate Inning

461. Who won the first World Series in 1903?

Boston Americans

462. Pumpsie Green played for which team?

Boston Red Sox

463. This player would keep four leaf clovers in his locker:

Sherm Lollar

464. Youngest player to hit 100 home runs?

Mel Ott

465. Craig Biggio was known to cover his bat with what?

Pine Tar

466. In what year did Whitey Ford throw 283 innings without allowing a single steal?

1961

467. Pitcher was known as a "Bonus Baby":

Sandy Koufax

468. You can find the "Pork Rind Chipper" at this ballpark:

Camden Yards

469. How many "Luxury Suites" does Yankee Stadium have?

56

470. You will find "Toasted Grasshoppers" served here:

Safeco Field

471. Which pitcher has the lowest E.R.A. at 1.82?

Ed Walsh

472. What does the acronym IP stand for?

Innings Pitched

473. He hit a grand slam on the first pitch he saw in big leagues:

Kevin Kouzmanoff

474. Fredbird is what type of bird?

Cardinal

475. Number of shutouts both Tom Seaver & Nolan Ryan tied for.

61

476. Wore #10 and was inducted to Hall of Fame his first year?

Chipper Jones

477. Who holds record for most RBIs?

Hank Aaron

478. The only stadium that sells more sausages than hot dogs:

Miller Park

479. What is the most popular type of grass used on MLB fields?

Kentucky Bluegrass

480. He decided to wear two mismatched socks:

Mark Teixeira

481. This player was thrown out 4 times trying to steal in one game in 1986:

Robby Thompson

482. He pitched consecutive no-hitters four days apart in 1938:

Johnny Vander Meer

483. What year did Ted Williams retire?

1960

484. Who was the youngest player to make a MLB debut in 1944?

Joe Nuxhall

485. David Ortiz always spit on what before an at-bat?

Batting Glove

486. What does the acronym ER stand for?

Earned Run

487. Who is not a pitcher in this set of names?

Hank Aaron

488. Holds record for most times caught stealing bases (335):

Rickey Henderson

489. What does HRR stand for?

Home Run Ratio

490. Come to Dodger Stadium to enjoy what?

Super Dodger Dog

491. Not featured on any mainstream baseball cards from 1954-1957:

Stan Musial

492. World Series first to have a game scheduled at night:

1971

493. How many total suites does Fenway Park have?

52

494. Which pitcher holds the record for most losses?

Cy Young

495. What are the Boston Red Sox' team colors ?

Red Hot & Blue Night

496. In 1912 this ballpark was completed:

Fenway Park

497. Monte Irvin played for which team?

New York Giants

498. SB stands for what?

Stolen Base

499. Who won Rookie of the Year in 2012 unanimously?

Mike Trout

500. Baseball field lines are made with what material?

Limestone

Made in the USA
Monee, IL
21 May 2022